CHOCOLATE BLISS

150 Easy Chocolate Recipes

BONNIE SCOTT

Graphics by Cheryl Seslar Designs

ISBN-13: 978-1537774558

CONTENTS

PIE

BARS

Chocolate Recipes

Who doesn't love chocolate? This universal ingredient is enjoyed in everything from chocolate cakes, cookies, bars and brownies to mousse, frosting, candy and puddings. Whether it's a dark, decadent, over-the-top main flavor or a subtle, secondary ingredient to accent other ingredients, you can't go wrong with chocolate.

Chocolate includes a wide variety of flavors. Sweet white chocolate is great for party mix and drop cookies. Delicate milk chocolate is perfect for the kids - pudding, cream pie, chocolate covered nuts and raisins are just right for light chocolate tastes.

Cocoa and unsweetened baking chocolate are perfect when blended into decadent cake and puddings, and semi-sweet chocolate chips are the natural add-in for the best cookies and bars to keep handy in the kitchen cookie jar.

Browse through this assortment of 150 delicious and decadent chocolate treats for inspiration any time your family has a chocolate craving. Whether it's an over-the-top dessert for guests or a quick and easy snack for movie night, you're sure to find the perfect recipe in Chocolate Bliss to satisfy your family's chocolate cravings!

ASSORTED CHOCOLATES

ASSORTED CHOCOLATES

Chocolate Cinnamon Rolls

3/4 cup warm water
1 package yeast
3/4 cup vegetable oil
1/2 teaspoon salt
1/3 cup cocoa
1 egg
2 1/4 cups all-purpose flour, divided
1/4 cup granulated sugar
Cinnamon
Butter

In a large bowl, dissolve yeast in warm water. Add vegetable oil, salt, cocoa, egg and 1 cup flour. Beat with electric mixer for 2 minutes at medium speed. Stir in remaining 1 1/4 cups flour and blend well. Let rise in warm place until doubled in size, about one hour.

Turn soft dough out on a well-floured board. Roll into a rectangle and spread with butter, cinnamon and sugar. Roll as a jelly roll and let rise until double in size. Bake in preheated oven at 350 degrees F. for 25 to 30 minutes. If desired, frost when cool.

Chocolate Reindeer Droppings

3 cups quick oats
1 cup coconut
2 cups granulated sugar
1/2 cup butter or margarine
1/3 cup cocoa
1/2 cup milk

In a medium saucepan, bring sugar, butter, cocoa and milk to a boil. Remove from heat; add oats and coconut. Mix well and drop by teaspoonfuls on wax paper. Refrigerate.

Chocolate Pizza

1 (12 oz.) package semi-sweet chocolate chips
1 lb. white almond bark, divided
2 cups mini marshmallows
1 cup peanuts
1 cup crisp rice cereal
1 (6 oz.) jar red maraschino cherries, drained and cut in half
3 tablespoons green maraschino cherries, drained and cut in quarters
1/3 cup coconut
1 teaspoon vegetable oil

Melt chocolate chips with 14 oz. almond bark in a 2-quart microwave dish; stir until smooth. Add mini marshmallows, nuts and cereal. Grease a 12-inch pizza pan; pour batter on pizza pan. Sprinkle with cherries and coconut.

Melt remaining 2 ounces almond bark with vegetable oil, stirring until smooth. Drizzle almond bark mixture over cherries and coconut. Chill until firm, store at room temperature.

Chocolate Orange Trifle Tower

8 oz. mascarpone cheese
1/4 cup granulated sugar
2 cups heavy whipping cream, divided
1/2 cup miniature chocolate chips
1 (10 oz.) jar orange curd
1 package chocolate wafer cookies
6 medium-size wine or parfait glasses

Beat mascarpone, sugar and 1 cup heavy whipping cream until thickened. Fold in chocolate chips; set aside. Whip remaining 1 cup of cream until soft peaks form. Fold in orange curd; set aside. Coarsely crush chocolate wafers.

To Assemble: In glasses, layer the orange curd mixture, mascarpone mixture, cookie crumbs; repeat and finish with an additional layer of mascarpone. Continue layering in remaining glasses.

Chocolate Covered Bacon

Thick-sliced hickory sweet bacon
1 cup milk chocolate chips
1 cup semi-sweet chocolate chips
2 tablespoons vegetable oil

Place bacon, in whole strips, on a foil-lined baking pan. Bake in preheated oven at 400 degrees F. for 25 to 30 minutes until crisp. (The bacon needs to be crisp but still pliable or it may break.) Remove and drain on paper towels until cool.

Combine semi-sweet chocolate chips and milk chocolate chips in a microwave-safe bowl. Add vegetable oil and stir. Microwave in 30 second increments on HIGH until melted. (If chocolate mixture seems too thick, thin it with a little more vegetable oil.) Dip bacon in chocolate or brush chocolate on bacon and lay on foil.

Chocolate Whip Cream Roll

6 eggs
1 cup granulated sugar, divided
1 teaspoon vanilla
1/2 teaspoon salt
4 tablespoons all-purpose flour
4 tablespoons cocoa
1/2 teaspoon cream of tartar
1 pint whipping cream
6 tablespoons confectioners' sugar
1 teaspoon vanilla

Separate eggs. In a medium bowl, beat egg yolks; add 1/2 cup granulated sugar and mix until thick. In another bowl, combine vanilla, salt, flour and cocoa; add to egg yolk mixture. Beat until well mixed. Set aside.

In a separate bowl, beat egg whites until foamy. Add cream of tartar and continue beating, add 1/2 cup granulated sugar and beat until peaks form. Gently fold egg whites into chocolate mixture. Pour into a well-greased 10x15-inch baking pan that is lined with parchment paper. Bake in preheated oven at 350 degrees F. for 20 to 25 minutes.

When done, turn out on a dish towel sprinkled with confectioners' sugar (do not use terrycloth). Gently remove parchment paper and roll in towel. Cool completely.

When cool gently unroll and spread with 1/2 pint whipping cream whipped with 3 tablespoons confectioners' sugar and 1/2 teaspoon vanilla. Reroll and cover with another 1/2 pint cream whipped the same way. Optional - Sprinkle with chocolate curls.

Yield: Serves 8.

Holiday Chocolate Pumpkin Bread

1 3/4 cups all-purpose flour
1 teaspoon cinnamon
1 teaspoon pumpkin pie spice
1/2 teaspoon nutmeg
1/2 teaspoon salt
1 teaspoon baking soda
1/2 cup butter
1 cup granulated sugar
2 eggs
1 1/2 cups canned pumpkin
3/4 cup chocolate chips
3/4 cup walnuts, divided

In a large bowl, combine flour, cinnamon, pumpkin pie spice, nutmeg, baking soda and salt. In another bowl, cream butter and sugar together. Blend in eggs and beat.

Add dry ingredients alternately with pumpkin to butter and sugar mixture. Mix in chocolate chips and 1/2 cup nuts. Grease bottom of a 9x5-inch loaf pan and pour batter in pan. Sprinkle 1/4 cup nuts on top. Bake in preheated oven at 350 degrees F. for 65 to 70 minutes. Cool then drizzle with glaze.

Glaze:
1/2 cup confectioners' sugar
1/8 teaspoon cinnamon
1/8 teaspoon nutmeg
1 to 2 tablespoons cream

Mix all glaze ingredients together; microwave for about 20 seconds. Mix well, then drizzle on bread.

Yield: 1 loaf.

Minis: This recipe will make 4 mini-loaves (fill pans 3/4 full with batter) baked for 40 to 45 minutes or until they pass the toothpick test.

Turtle Pie Dessert

1 package brownie mix
1/2 gallon butter crunch, caramel, or chocolate ice cream
1 cup pecans, chopped
1 cup semi-sweet chocolate chips
1/2 cup butter
2 cups confectioners' sugar
1 1/2 cups evaporated milk
1 teaspoon vanilla

Prepare brownie mix as directed. Bake in preheated oven at 350 degrees F. in a 9x13-inch pan for 25 minutes; cool.

When cool, spread ice cream over brownies. Sprinkle pecans over ice cream and freeze. Cook chocolate chips, butter, confectioners' sugar, evaporated milk and vanilla over medium heat until thick (approximately 20 minutes). Cool syrup and drizzle over ice cream; keep frozen.

White Chocolate Party Mix

10 oz. package mini-pretzels
5 cups Cheerios
5 cups Crispix, or corn or rice Chex cereal
2 cups mixed nuts or peanuts
1 lb. M & M's
2-12 oz. pkgs. vanilla chips
3 tablespoons vegetable oil

In a large bowl, combine pretzels, Cheerios, Chex cereal, nuts and M&M's. Melt vanilla chips and oil in microwave. Stir until melted and smooth. Pour over cereal mixture. Mix well and spread on waxed paper. Cool. Store in airtight container.

Tortilla Torte

2 (12 oz. each) pkgs. milk chocolate chips
6 cups sour cream, divided
3/4 cup confectioners' sugar
10 12-inch flour tortillas
Shaved bittersweet chocolate

Melt chocolate and mix with 4 cups sour cream. In another bowl, mix sugar and remaining 2 cups sour cream.

On a plate large enough to hold tortillas, layer 8 tortillas with chocolate mixture. It will take about 1/2 cup chocolate mixture to cover each tortilla. Add the ninth tortilla and cover with most of the sugar mixture. Add the last tortilla and spread remaining sugar mixture evenly over the top, covering all edges.

Cover tortillas with a large bowl or other covering that does not touch surface. Refrigerate for at least 12 hours. Decorate with shaved chocolate and cut into small wedges to serve this very rich dessert.

Yield: 20 servings.

Chocolate Sundae Dessert

2/3 cup butter or margarine
2 cups confectioners' sugar
3 (1 oz.) pkgs. unsweetened chocolate (pre-melted)
3 eggs
1 teaspoon vanilla
1 cup walnuts, broken
1 package Nabisco famous chocolate wafer cookies, crushed
1 tablespoon butter or margarine, melted
1/2 gallon vanilla ice cream

Cream butter or margarine and confectioners' sugar; add unsweetened chocolate, eggs, vanilla and nuts.

Line bottom of an 8x11-inch baking pan with crushed wafer cookies mixed with 1 tablespoon melted margarine. Put chocolate mixture on top of crumbs evenly. Layer vanilla ice cream on top and sprinkle with a few reserved cookie crumbs. Freeze overnight.

Yield: Serves 15.

Chocolate Peppermint Dessert

1 (15.25 oz.) package Oreo cookies
1 cup butter
4 cups confectioners' sugar
4 (1 oz. each) semi-sweet chocolate baking squares
6 eggs
1/2 gallon peppermint ice cream

Crush Oreo cookies with cream filling into a 9x13-inch baking pan, reserving 1/4 cup.

Cream butter with confectioners' sugar. Add melted chocolate and 6 beaten egg yolks. Add 6 beaten egg whites with a little of sugar added. Pour over cookie crumbs in pan and freeze. When frozen, add ice cream and cover with remaining crumbs.

Yield: Serves 18.

Chocolate Fondue

2 cups light corn syrup
24 oz. milk chocolate chips
1 tablespoon vanilla
1/2 cup heavy cream
Optional - Brandy or rum

In a large saucepan, combine corn syrup and chocolate chips. Over low heat, stir until chocolate melts and mixture is smooth. Add vanilla (omit if using brandy or rum) and cream. Add optional brandy or rum. Stir until blended.

Keep warm in fondue pot. Dip fruit or pound cake, cut into bite-size pieces. Suggestions: Strawberries, pineapple, mandarin oranges, bananas.

Oreo Cookie Dessert

1 small package Oreo cookies (crushed)
1/2 gallon vanilla ice cream
1 jar chocolate fudge sauce
Peanuts, chopped
1 carton refrigerated whipped topping

Layer Oreo cookie crumbs in 9x13-inch baking pan. Cut ice cream into 1/2 inch slices and layer on top of cookie crumbs. Top with fudge sauce. Sprinkle peanut crumbs over fudge. Spread whipped topping over the top. Sprinkle any remaining cookie crumbs on top and freeze.

Chocolate Almond Velvet

1 (16 oz.) can chocolate syrup
1 (14 oz.) can sweetened condensed milk
2 pints whipping cream
2 teaspoons vanilla extract
1/2 cup slivered almonds, toasted

In a large bowl, combine chocolate syrup, condensed milk, whipping cream and vanilla; beat until stiff peaks form. Fold in almonds. Spread into an ungreased 13x9x2-inch baking dish. Cover and freeze for 4 hours or until firm. Remove from freezer 5 minutes before serving.

Yield: 16 to 20 servings.

Chocolate Layer Dessert

Crust:

1 cup all-purpose flour
1/2 cup butter, melted
1/2 cup nuts, chopped

Filling:

1 (8 oz.) package cream cheese
1 cup confectioners' sugar
1 (8 oz.) carton refrigerated whipped topping
1 large package instant chocolate pudding

For Crust: In a medium bowl, combine flour, melted butter and chopped nuts. Press the mixture into a 9x13-inch baking pan. Bake in preheated oven at 350 degrees F. for 20 minutes. Allow to cool.

For Filling: Beat cream cheese and confectioners' sugar together. Add 1/2 of the whipped topping. Spread the cream cheese mixture on baked crust.

Prepare instant chocolate pudding as directed on box. Spread pudding over the cream cheese mixture. Top with the remaining 1/2 package of whipped topping and sprinkle with chopped nuts.

Chocolate Pretzels

15 small square pretzels
15 chocolate kisses with caramel, unwrapped
15 M&M's

Line a cookie sheet with foil. Place pretzels on foil and center an unwrapped chocolate kiss on the pretzel. Bake in preheated oven at 275 degrees F. for 2 minutes.

Immediately press an M&M in the center of each kiss, pressing down gently so the chocolate kiss spreads out. Refrigerate for 15 minutes until chocolate hardens, then store at room temperature.

Chocolate Passion Dessert

24 fudge brownies
2 cups sliced strawberries, fresh or frozen
2 bananas
2 (8 oz.) cartons refrigerated whipped topping, thawed*
3 tablespoons chocolate syrup

*To make chocolate whipped topping, add about 3 tablespoons chocolate syrup to whipped topping and beat well.

Cut brownies into 1/2-inch pieces. Layer in a 3-quart serving bowl: 1/2 of brownies, 1 cup strawberries, 1 sliced banana and 8 oz. whipped topping. Repeat layers. Refrigerate until ready to serve.

Yield: 16 servings.

Chocolate Angel Mousse Dessert

1 8" or 9" baked angel food cake
3 cups semi-sweet chocolate chips, melted
3 eggs
1 (12 oz.) carton refrigerated whipped topping
1/2 cup semi-sweet chocolate chips, melted for drizzle

Spray 8-inch spring-form pan with non-stick cooking spray. Melt 3 cups chocolate chips over low heat in double boiler. Add eggs, one at a time, and stir into chocolate mixture. Cook and stir for one minute; cool. Add 1 pint of whipped topping to cooled chocolate mixture.

Cube the angel food cake. Begin layering in pan: cake, chocolate mixture, cake, chocolate mixture. Cover with foil. Refrigerate 24 hours. Loosen pan and turn out on plate. Frost with whipped topping and fluff to form peaks. Drizzle with melted chocolate chips; slice.

Brownies

BROWNIES

Applesauce Brownies

1 1/2 cups granulated sugar
1/2 cup butter
2 eggs
2 tablespoons cocoa
1/2 teaspoon salt
1 teaspoon baking soda
2 cups all-purpose flour
1/2 teaspoon cinnamon
2 cups applesauce
1/2 cup mini chocolate chips

In a medium saucepan, melt sugar and butter; remove from heat and beat in eggs; stir in cocoa and salt.

In a medium bowl, mix together baking soda, flour and cinnamon and add alternately with applesauce to the sugar mixture. Spread in greased and floured 10x15-inch cookie sheet (jelly roll pan). Bake in preheated oven at 350 degrees F. for 30 minutes. Sprinkle immediately with chocolate chips.

Chocolate Syrup Brownies

1/2 cup margarine
1 cup granulated sugar
4 eggs
1 (16 oz.) can chocolate syrup
1 cup + 1 tablespoon all-purpose flour
1/2 teaspoon baking powder
1/2 cup walnuts, chopped

In a large bowl, cream together margarine and sugar. Add eggs, 2 at a time, beating well. Add chocolate syrup alternately with flour and baking powder. Fold in nuts. Pour into a 9x13-inch baking pan. Bake in preheated oven at 350 degrees for 30 minutes.

Frosting:

6 tablespoons milk
1 1/2 cups granulated sugar
6 tablespoons margarine
1/2 cup semi-sweet chocolate chips

Boil milk, sugar and margarine for 30 seconds, remove from heat and add chocolate chips. Beat and spread on warm brownies.

Yield: Serves 30.

Chocolate Chip Brownies

11 graham crackers, crushed
6 oz. semi-sweet chocolate chips
3/4 cup nuts, chopped
1 (14 oz.) can sweetened condensed milk

In a large mixing bowl, combine all ingredients and mix thoroughly. Pour into greased 9-inch square pan. Bake in preheated oven at 375 degrees F. for approximately 20 minutes. Cool before cutting.

Frosted Brownies

1 cup margarine, melted
2 cups granulated sugar
4 eggs
2 teaspoons vanilla
1 1/2 cups all-purpose flour
1/2 cup cocoa
1 cup walnuts, chopped

In a large bowl, cream margarine and sugar together. Add eggs and vanilla. Mix together flour and cocoa; stir into sugar mixture. Add nuts and stir just until mixed. Pour into a 9x13-inch baking pan. Bake in preheated oven at 350 degrees for 25 to 30 minutes.

Frosting:

3 tablespoons margarine, melted
3 tablespoons milk
3/4 cup granulated sugar
1/4 cup semi-sweet chocolate chips

In a medium saucepan, mix together margarine, milk and sugar. Bring to a boil and boil for 30 seconds. Add chocolate chips. Mix well. Spread while warm.

Mint Brownies

4 (1 oz. each) squares unsweetened chocolate
1 cup margarine
4 eggs
2 cups granulated sugar
1/2 teaspoon peppermint extract
1 cup all-purpose flour
1/8 teaspoon salt

In a medium saucepan, melt chocolate and margarine. In a large bowl, beat eggs until frothy. Stir in chocolate mixture and sugar. Add peppermint extract, flour and salt. Mix well and pour into greased 9x13-inch baking pan. Bake in preheated oven at 350 degrees for 30 minutes.

Frosting:
4 tablespoons margarine
2 cups confectioners' sugar
2 tablespoons milk
1 1/2 teaspoons peppermint extract

In a medium bowl, beat together margarine, confectioners' sugar, milk and peppermint extract. Spread over cooled brownies and refrigerate until solid.

Topping:
1 square bitter chocolate
1 tablespoon margarine

Melt chocolate and margarine together; dribble over frosting. Refrigerate until cool and cut into squares.

Yield: 36 pieces.

Caramel Brownies

1 (16.5 oz.) package German chocolate cake mix
3/4 cup butter or margarine
1 (5 oz.) can evaporated milk
12 oz. semi-sweet chocolate chips
1 (11 oz.) bag caramels

In a medium bowl, stir cake mix, butter or margarine and 1/2 can evaporated milk together. Place 1/2 of mixture into a 9x13-inch baking pan. Sprinkle chocolate chips on top. Bake in preheated oven at 350 degrees F. for 6 minutes.

In a medium saucepan, melt caramels and remaining 1/2 can evaporated milk. Pour over baked mixture. Add remaining mix and spread evenly. Bake in preheated oven at 350 degrees F. for 16 minutes.

Easy No Bake Brownies

4 cups graham cracker crumbs
1 cup walnuts, chopped
1/2 cup confectioners' sugar
2 cups semi-sweet chocolate chips
1 cup evaporated milk
1 teaspoon vanilla

In a large bowl, combine cracker crumbs, nuts and confectioners' sugar. In a saucepan, melt chocolate chips in evaporated milk over low heat; stir constantly. Add vanilla.

Reserve 1/2 cup of chocolate mixture and stir remaining chocolate mixture into crumb mixture. Spread in buttered 9x9" pan. Spread the remaining 1/2 cup chocolate mixture over the top. Chill.

Yield: 2 1/2 dozen.

Chocolate Brownies

2 cups granulated sugar
1 1/2 cups all-purpose flour
1/4 cup cocoa
1 teaspoon salt
1 cup vegetable oil
4 eggs
2 teaspoons vanilla
1/2 cup nuts

In a large bowl, combine all ingredients. Beat at a medium speed for 2 minutes. Pour in a greased 10 1/2 x 15 1/2-inch jelly roll pan. Bake in preheated oven at 350 degrees F. for 20 to 25 minutes. Frost when cool.

Yield: 32 pieces.

Coffee Brownies

2 1/2 cups brown sugar, packed
3/4 cup butter or margarine
2 teaspoons strong instant coffee granules
1 teaspoon hot water
2 eggs
2 teaspoons vanilla
2 cups all-purpose flour
2 teaspoons baking powder
1/2 teaspoon salt
1 cup pecans, chopped
1 cup chocolate chips

In a medium saucepan, melt brown sugar and butter or margarine over medium heat until melted, stirring constantly. Dissolve coffee granules in hot water; blend into sugar mixture and let cool. Beat in eggs and vanilla.

In a separate bowl, combine flour, baking powder and salt; stir flour mixture into sugar mixture. Stir in pecans and chocolate chips. Spread in a greased 9x13" baking dish. Bake in preheated oven at 350 degrees F. for 30 minutes.

Yield: 2 dozen.

Candy

CANDY

Toffee Fudge

1 cup pecans, chopped
3/4 cup brown sugar, packed
1/2 cup butter
4 1/2 oz. milk chocolate bar, cut in pieces

Sprinkle pecans on bottom of greased 9-inch square baking pan. Combine brown sugar and butter in a saucepan. Bring to a boil, stirring constantly; boil for 7 minutes. Remove from heat; spread over nuts.

Sprinkle chocolate pieces over top. When chocolate melts, spread evenly. Refrigerate until cold. Turn entire pan out at once and break into pieces of desired size. Chocolate chips may be substituted for milk chocolate.

Peanut Butter Chocolate Fudge

1 (7 oz.) jar marshmallow cream
1 1/2 cups granulated sugar
2/3 cup evaporated milk
1/4 cup butter or margarine
1/4 teaspoon salt
1 cup peanut butter chips
1 cup semi-sweet chocolate chips
1 teaspoon vanilla

In a large saucepan, mix together marshmallow cream, sugar, evaporated milk, butter or margarine and salt. Over medium heat, bring to a rolling boil, stirring constantly. Boil for 5 minutes.

Remove from heat; add peanut butter chips and chocolate chips. Stir in vanilla. Pour into a buttered 8-inch square pan and chill until firm.

Microwave Fudge

18 oz. package semi-sweet chocolate chips
1 (14 oz.) can sweetened condensed milk
1 teaspoon vanilla
1 1/2 cups pecans

In a microwave-safe bowl, mix chocolate chips and condensed milk together; microwave for one minute on High. Stir, microwave 1 1/2 minutes more. Add vanilla and pecans; mix well. Pour in an 8x8" buttered dish and refrigerate.

Chocolate Covered Cherries

1 lb. confectioners' sugar
1/3 cup light corn syrup
1/3 cup butter or margarine
1/4 teaspoon salt
1 teaspoon vanilla
1 (10 oz.) jar maraschino cherries
1 (6 oz.) package semi-sweet chocolate chips
1/2 square of paraffin or vegetable oil

In a medium bowl, mix sugar, corn syrup, butter or margarine, salt and vanilla thoroughly (works best to use hands).

Cut cherries in half. Shape some mixture around each cherry half; chill well. Melt chocolate chips over hot water; add a little paraffin or oil. Drop candies into chocolate to coat; refrigerate.

Peanut Crispies

1/2 cup butter or margarine
12 oz. package semi-sweet chocolate chips
2 lbs. marshmallows
1 (12 oz.) can of peanuts, ground
4 1/2 cups crispy rice cereal

Over low to medium heat, melt butter or margarine in heavy 3 quart saucepan. Add chocolate chips and marshmallows.

Remove from heat. Add peanuts and cereal. Stir until mixed thoroughly. Pour into well-buttered 15 1/2 x 17 1/2-inch baking pan and let cool.

Yield: 36 pieces.

Chocolate Drops

1/2 cup vegetable oil
1 2/3 cups granulated sugar
2 teaspoons vanilla
2 eggs
2 (1 oz. each) squares unsweetened chocolate, melted
1/2 cup confectioners' sugar
2 cups all-purpose flour
2 teaspoons baking powder
1/2 teaspoon salt
1/3 cup milk
1/2 cup nuts

In a large bowl, cream vegetable oil, granulated sugar and vanilla. Beat eggs. Add to creamed mixture. Add melted chocolate.

In another bowl, mix together confectioners' sugar, flour, baking powder and salt. Add alternately with milk to creamed mixture. Blend well. Stir in nuts.

Chill dough 2 to 3 hours, or overnight. Form into small balls about 1 inch. Roll in confectioners' sugar. Place on greased cookie sheet. Bake in preheated oven at 350 degrees for 20 minutes.

Rocky Road Candy

8 oz. milk chocolate
8 oz. semi-sweet chocolate (1 1/3 cup)
16 marshmallows (or 2 cups mini marshmallows)
3/4 cup nuts

Melt milk chocolate and semi-sweet chocolate over hot water. Spread 1/4 inch thick in an 8x8-inch buttered pan (about half of the chocolate). Pour marshmallows and nuts over chocolate mixture. Add the rest of the chocolate mixture on top. Chill and cut into 6 squares.

Chocolate Rum Balls

1 (6 oz.) package semi-sweet chocolate morsels
1 (7 oz.) jar marshmallow cream
1 tablespoon imitation rum extract
3 cups crispy rice cereal
1/2 cup pecans, chopped
1/2 cup shredded coconut

Place chocolate chips in top of a double boiler; bring water to a boil. Reduce heat to low; cook until chocolate melts. Cool.

In a medium bowl, blend melted chocolate, marshmallow cream, and rum extract; stir well. Add cereal, pecans and coconut to chocolate mixture, stirring just until well-combined. Shape into 1" balls. Chill until firm.

Yield: 4 1/2 dozen.

Old-Fashioned Millionaires

1 (14 oz.) package caramels
3 or 4 tablespoons milk
2 cups pecan pieces
Margarine (for waxed paper)
1 tablespoon vegetable oil
1 (12 oz.) package semi-sweet chocolate morsels

Melt caramels in milk over low heat; stir in pecans. Drop by teaspoonful onto buttered waxed paper. Chill.

Melt vegetable oil and chocolate morsels in a heavy saucepan over low heat. Remove from heat; dip candy into chocolate, and return to waxed paper. Refrigerate.

Yield: 3 1/2 dozen.

Chocolate-Covered Raisins

1/4 cup dark corn syrup
1 (6 oz.) package semi-sweet chocolate chips
2 cup raisins
2 tablespoons confectioners' sugar
1 1/2 teaspoons vanilla extract

In top of a double boiler, combine corn syrup and chocolate chips; bring water to a boil. Reduce heat to low; cook until chocolate melts, stirring constantly. Remove from heat.

Add raisins, confectioners' sugar and vanilla; stir until mixed. Drop by half-teaspoonful onto waxed paper; chill. Store in refrigerator.

Yield: 5 1/2 dozen.

Chocolate Ting-A-Lings

1 (12 oz.) package semi-sweet chocolate chips
4 cups corn flakes

Melt chocolate chips; cool to room temperature. Gently stir in corn flakes until well coated. Drop by spoonfuls onto waxed paper or foil. Refrigerate until set, about 2 hours.

Chocolate Caramels

1 cup granulated sugar
1 cup brown sugar, packed
1/2 cup corn syrup
1/2 cup half-and-half
2 (1 oz. each) squares unsweetened chocolate
2 tablespoons butter or margarine, cut in pieces
1 teaspoon vanilla

Place sugar and brown sugar, corn syrup, half-and-half, and chocolate in large heavy saucepan. Bring to a boil, stirring to melt chocolate and dissolve sugar. Reduce heat to medium and continue cooking, stirring occasionally, until syrup reaches 248 degrees F. on candy thermometer (firm-ball stage). Remove from heat.

Quickly stir in butter or margarine and vanilla just until blended and butter melts. Pour into well-greased 8x8x2-inch baking pan. Cool. Cut in small squares. If desired, top each square with pecan halves or almond slivers. Wrap individually in plastic wrap or foil. Store in cool, dry place.

Yield: 1 1/2 pounds.

Sweetheart Chocolate Truffles

6 oz. semi-sweet chocolate
1 ounce unsweetened chocolate
1/2 cup whipping cream
2 tablespoons butter
3/4 cup confectioners' sugar
2 egg yolks
1 to 2 tablespoons rum, brandy or favorite liqueur
Cocoa, chopped nuts, colored nonpareils, finely grated chocolate

Finely chopped raisins or nuts may be added to chocolate before chilling.

Combine chocolate, whipping cream and butter in top of double boiler. Stir over hot water to melt chocolate. Remove from heat.

Cover chocolate surface with confectioners' sugar. Top with egg yolks. Whisk until smooth, returning to heat to thoroughly blend ingredients. Remove from heat. Add liqueur. Pour into flat dish and refrigerate until chilled. Shape into small balls, roll in cocoa, nuts, etc. Refrigerate until shortly before serving. Serve in paper candy cups.

Yield: 3 to 4 dozen.

Easy Chocolate Truffles

1 1/2 lb. milk chocolate
1/3 cup heavy cream
1/3 cup half and half
1 1/2 teaspoons vanilla extract

Melt milk chocolate in double boiler over hot water; beat until smooth.

In a saucepan, bring cream and half and half just to the simmering point. Cool to 130 degrees F. Add to melted chocolate; beat until smooth. Stir in vanilla. Cool. Beat until light and fluffy.

Chill until firm. Shape into small balls. If desired, dip into melted dipping chocolate or roll in cocoa.

Chocolate Surprises

1 (14 oz.) can sweetened condensed milk
2 squares chocolate
1/4 teaspoon salt
1 teaspoon vanilla
1 cup chopped nuts
3 cups shredded coconut

In a saucepan over low heat, heat milk and chocolate together with salt. When completely melted, remove from heat and add nuts and coconut. Mix well.

Drop by spoonfuls onto cookie sheet. Bake in preheated oven at 375 degrees F. for 10 minutes.

Turtles

28 caramels
2 tablespoons cream
1 cup pecans
3 chocolate bars, melted over warm water

Melt caramels with cream in a double boiler. When creamy, add pecans and let cool. Drop by teaspoonful on waxed paper. Shape with spoon and frost each turtle with melted chocolate. Do not refrigerate. Make each turtle small, as they are very rich.

Tiger Butter Candy

1 (24 oz.) package almond bark
1/2 cup crunchy peanut butter
1 1/2 cups semi-sweet chocolate chips

Line a cookie sheet with aluminum foil. In a saucepan, melt almond bark and peanut butter together over low heat. While that is melting, melt the chocolate chips in a microwave at 50% power, stirring every 30 seconds.

When melted, pour the almond bark mixture on the foil lined cookie sheet. Drizzle the melted chocolate chips over the almond bark mixture and make swirly designs with a spoon. Refrigerate until cold; break into pieces.

Coconut Swirls

2 tablespoons butter
3 tablespoons water
1 teaspoon vanilla
2 cups confectioners' sugar
1/2 cup instant dry milk
3 cups coconut
12 oz. semi-sweet chocolate chips

Melt butter in a medium saucepan. Remove from heat; add water and vanilla.

In a bowl, combine sugar and instant milk. Add to butter mixture, about 1/2 cup at a time, mixing well after each addition. Stir in coconut. Drop by teaspoonfuls onto waxed paper. Let stand until firm - about 10 minutes. Melt chocolate chips over hot (not boiling) water or in microwave. Swirl a teaspoon of melted chocolate on top of each candy, then refrigerate.

Yield: 36 candies.

Peanut Clusters

1 pound almond bark (white)
1 (12 oz.) package semi-sweet chocolate chips
1 (12 oz.) jar dry roasted peanuts

Melt almond bark in double broiler or microwave at 50% power. Add chocolate chips and stir until melted. Add peanuts.

Cool and beat until a little firm; drop by spoonfuls onto waxed paper. Cool and store in tins.

White Chocolate Peppermint Brittle

30 small peppermint candy canes or 4 regular candy canes
2 pounds white chocolate

In a microwave-safe dish, melt white chocolate in microwave, stirring every 30 seconds.

Break candy canes into small pieces. (Putting the candy canes in a couple of resealable plastic bags and smashing them with a rolling pin or hammer works well.) Add most of the candy cane pieces to the melted chocolate; stir to mix.

Spread mixture thinly on a wax paper or parchment paper lined cookie sheet. Sprinkle the remaining candy cane pieces on top, along with the "peppermint dust". Refrigerate until hard, about 30 minutes. Break into pieces.

Raisin Pecan Chewies

1 (12 oz.) package milk chocolate chips
1/2 teaspoon vanilla
1 1/2 cups golden raisins
1/2 cup pecans, chopped
1 cup corn flakes

In a medium saucepan, melt chocolate chips over low heat, stirring until melted or microwave for about 2 minutes, stirring every 30 seconds. Remove from heat; stir in vanilla, raisins, pecans, and corn flakes. Drop by teaspoon on waxed paper-lined cookie sheets. Refrigerate until firm.

Yield: 40 candies.

PIES

PIE

Grasshopper Pie

8 or 9-inch chocolate pie crust or 14 Oreo cookies, crushed
2 tablespoons butter or margarine, melted

Combine Oreo cookies and butter or margarine. Press into an 8" pie pan.

24 marshmallows
1/2 cup milk
3 tablespoons crème de menthe
2 tablespoons crème de cocoa
1 cup cream, whipped

In a saucepan over low heat, melt marshmallows in milk. Stir in crème de menthe and crème de cocoa. Remove from heat; cool and add whipped cream. Pour into crust. Chill.

Yield: 1 pie.

Chocolate Chess Pie

2 1/2 cups granulated sugar
2/3 cup evaporated milk
4 tablespoons butter or margarine
1 teaspoon vanilla
4 or 5 eggs
4 tablespoons cocoa (or 2 (1 oz. each) squares
unsweetened chocolate)
1/4 teaspoon salt
2 unbaked 8 or 9-inch pie shells

Mix all ingredients together in order and put in 2 unbaked pie shells. Bake in preheated oven at 350 degrees F. for 45 minutes.

Yield: 2 pies.

Chocolate Cream Pie

8 or 9-inch graham cracker pie crust, baked
1 (6 oz.) package instant chocolate pudding
2/3 cup milk
1/3 of 1/2 gallon vanilla ice cream
Whipping cream
Chocolate candy bar

In a large bowl, let ice cream set until softened. Add milk and pudding to ice cream. Mix thoroughly. Pour into pie crust. When set, whip cream and spread on top. Grate chocolate bar onto the whipped topping. Keep refrigerated.

Yield: 1 pie.

Chocolate Truffle Pie

8 or 9-inch chocolate crumb pie crust
1/3 cup cold orange juice
1 envelope unflavored gelatin
1 tablespoon instant coffee
1 (6 oz.) package semi-sweet chocolate chips
1 teaspoon vanilla extract
2 eggs
1/4 cup granulated sugar
1 1/2 cups heavy or whipping cream, whipped*

Pour cold orange juice into a medium saucepan; sprinkle gelatin on top and let stand for 1 minute. Over low heat, stir constantly until gelatin is dissolved. Add instant coffee and chocolate, and heat, stirring constantly, until chocolate is thoroughly melted.

Remove from heat and stir in vanilla; let stand 10 minutes, or until lukewarm. Meanwhile, in large bowl, with electric mixer at high speed, beat eggs with sugar for 5 minutes, or until thickened. Gradually add lukewarm gelatin mixture, and beat until just thoroughly blended. Fold in whipped cream and chocolate shavings.

*Substitution: Use 2 cups frozen whipped topping, thawed.

Yield: 8 servings.

Mint Chocolate Mini-Pies

2 cups confectioners' sugar
1 cup butter
4 (1 oz.) squares unsweetened chocolate, melted
4 eggs
1 teaspoon peppermint flavoring
2 teaspoons vanilla
18 vanilla wafers
1 cup heavy cream whipped
1/2 cup pecan pieces
18 maraschino cherries
18 paper cupcake liners

In a large bowl, cream sugar and butter until fluffy and light. Add melted chocolate. Add eggs and beat well; mix in peppermint flavoring and vanilla.

Put a vanilla wafer in the bottom of paper cupcake liners. Fill with chocolate mixture 3/4 full. Add a dollop of whipped cream on top. Sprinkle with pecans and place a cherry on top. Freeze in muffin tins to keep shape. Serve frozen.

Yield: 18 mini-pies.

French Silk Chocolate Pie

1 1/8 cups granulated sugar
3/4 cup butter or margarine
2 packets liquid chocolate (bitter)
1 teaspoon vanilla
3 eggs
8 or 9-inch graham cracker or pie shell, baked

In a medium bowl, cream sugar and butter or margarine well, blend in liquid chocolate and vanilla. Add eggs, one at a time, beat 5 minutes after each at high speed. Pour into graham cracker or baked pie shell. Chill in refrigerator at least 6 hours before serving.

Yield: 1 pie.

Chocolate-Pecan Pie

1/4 lb. butter or margarine
3/4 cup granulated sugar
1 square chocolate, melted
1 teaspoon vanilla
2 eggs
1/2 cup pecans
8 or 9-inch. baked pie shell
Whipped cream

Cream butter or margarine; add sugar and chocolate. Beat well. Add vanilla and 1 egg; beat 5 minutes. Add remaining egg; beat 5 minutes. Stir in pecans. Place in pie shell; cool 2 hours or longer. Top with whipped cream. Can be frozen.

Yield: 6 servings.

Cheesy Chocolate Pie

2 (3 oz.) packages cream cheese, softened
1 cup granulated sugar
1 teaspoon vanilla
1/3 cup cocoa
1/3 cup milk
1 (8 oz.) carton refrigerated whipped topping
8 or 9-inch graham cracker crust

In a large bowl, combine cream cheese, sugar and vanilla until well blended. Add cocoa and milk, and blend. Fold in whipped topping. Pour into graham cracker crust.

Chocolate Mocha Pie

8 or 9-inch chocolate wafer crust
16 large marshmallows
1/2 cup milk
1 cup semi-sweet chocolate chips
1 tablespoon coffee powder
1/8 teaspoon salt
1 teaspoon vanilla
1 cup whipping cream

In a saucepan, heat marshmallows, milk, chocolate chips, coffee powder and salt over medium heat until smooth and well blended, stirring constantly. Add vanilla; chill until thickened.

Beat whipping cream until stiff; fold into chocolate mixture. Pour into crust and chill for 2 hours before serving. Serve with whipped cream.

Yield: 8 servings.

BARS

BARS

Chocolate Crunch Bars

1/2 cup margarine or butter
2 tablespoons cocoa
3/4 cup granulated sugar
2 eggs
1 teaspoon vanilla
3/4 cup all-purpose flour
1/2 teaspoon baking powder
1/2 cup nuts
10 oz. bag of miniature marshmallows

Combine all ingredients except marshmallows, and bake in preheated oven in a 9x13-inch baking pan at 350 degrees for 15 minutes. Spread with a half bag of marshmallows on top; bake 3 minutes longer.

Frosting:
1 cup semi-sweet chocolate chips
1/2 cup peanut butter
1 1/2 cups Special K cereal

Mix chocolate chips, peanut butter and cereal together. Frost cooled bars.

Crispy Chocolate Squares

30 regular size marshmallows
1/2 cup margarine or butter
1 teaspoon vanilla
5 cups Rice Krispies
1 cup semi-sweet chocolate chips, divided

In a medium saucepan, heat marshmallows and margarine or butter until melted. Stir in vanilla.

In a large bowl, combine Rice Krispies and 1/2 cup chocolate chips. Add marshmallow mixture to cereal mixture. Stir quickly until coated.

Spray a 9x13-inch baking pan with nonstick cooking spray. Pat mixture into pan. Melt remaining chocolate chips and drizzle over cereal. Chill until firm.

Snicker Bars

2 cups semi-sweet chocolate chips, divided
1/2 cup butterscotch chips, divided
1/2 cup peanut butter, divided
1 cup granulated sugar
1/4 cup milk
1/4 cup margarine or butter
1 (7 oz. tub) marshmallow cream
1/4 cup peanut butter
1 teaspoon vanilla
1 1/2 cups dry roasted peanuts, chopped
40 caramels
1 tablespoon heavy cream

Melt 1 cup chocolate chips, 1/4 cup butterscotch chips and 1/4 cup peanut butter together in microwave or on stovetop. Spray a 9x13-inch baking pan with nonstick cooking spray. Spread mixture in baking pan. Let cool.

In a medium saucepan, combine sugar, milk and margarine or butter. Over medium-high heat, bring to a boil and boil for 5 minutes, stirring constantly. Remove from heat; add marshmallow cream, peanut butter, vanilla and peanuts. Spread over first layer.

Melt caramels and heavy cream together in microwave or on stovetop; spread over second layer.

Melt together remaining 1 cup chocolate chips, 1/4 cup butterscotch chips and 1/4 cup peanut butter and spread over third layer. Cut into squares when set.

Seven Layer Bars

1/2 cup butter
1 cup graham cracker crumbs
1 cup coconut
1 cup semi-sweet chocolate chips
1 cup butterscotch chips
1 (14 oz.) can sweetened condensed milk
1 1/2 cup chopped walnuts

Melt butter and place it in a 9x13-inch baking pan. Add the remaining ingredients one at a time in order of above so there are seven layers. Bake in preheated oven at 350 degrees F. for 25 to 30 minutes.

Buttermilk Chocolate Bars

1/2 cup butter or margarine
1/2 cup vegetable oil
1 cup water
2 cups granulated sugar
2 cups all-purpose flour
1/4 cup cocoa
2 eggs
1/2 cup buttermilk
1 1/2 teaspoons baking soda
1 teaspoon vanilla

Bring butter or margarine, vegetable oil and water to a boil in a small saucepan. In a large bowl, mix sugar, flour and cocoa. Pour boiling mixture over flour mixture and beat until smooth. Add eggs. Beat again. Stir baking soda into the buttermilk; add to batter. Add vanilla and stir again. Pour into greased jellyroll pan (10 1/2 x 15 1/2 x 1). Bake in preheated oven at 350 degrees F. for 20 to 25 minutes.

Chocolate Frosting:

1 cup granulated sugar
1/4 cup margarine
1/4 cup milk
1 cup semi-sweet chocolate chips

Mix sugar, margarine and milk in a saucepan; boil for 1 minute, stirring constantly. Remove from heat and add chocolate chips. Beat until creamy. Spread on cake.

3-Layer No-Bake Chocolate Bars

Bottom Layer:

1/2 cup margarine or butter, softened
1 egg
5 tablespoons granulated sugar
3 tablespoons cocoa
1 teaspoon vanilla
2 cups crushed vanilla wafers
1 cup flaked coconut
1/2 cup nuts, chopped

Combine margarine or butter, egg, sugar, cocoa and vanilla in bowl. Set in a pan of hot water and stir until margarine melts and mixture appears to have consistency of custard. Mix together crushed vanilla wafers, coconut and nuts; add to cocoa mixture. Press into a greased 11x7-inch baking pan.

Second Layer:

4 tablespoons margarine or butter
2 tablespoons vanilla pudding mix (not instant)
3 tablespoons milk
2 cups confectioners' sugar

Cream margarine or butter; mix in pudding mix, milk and sugar and spread over chocolate base. Allow to harden in refrigerator.

Top Layer:

1 tablespoon margarine
1 (8 oz.) milk chocolate candy bar

Melt chocolate and margarine slowly over hot water and spread on top of hardened white layer. Cut when chocolate is set. Refrigerate. Cut into small pieces.

Ten Dollar Bars

1 cup peanut butter
1 cup butter
2 cups crushed graham crackers
2 cups confectioners' sugar
2 cups chocolate chips

Combine peanut butter, butter, graham crackers and confectioners' sugar. Press into buttered 9 x 13" pan. Melt chips in microwave and spread over the top. Chill before cutting and serving.

Oh Henry Bars

1 cup corn syrup
1 cup granulated sugar
1 1/2 cups peanut butter
1 1/2 cups corn flakes
3/4 (12 oz.) package semi-sweet chocolate chips
3/4 (12 oz.) package butterscotch chips

In a large saucepan, melt corn syrup, sugar and peanut butter. Stir over medium-high heat until mixture bubbles. Remove pan from stove. Add corn flakes; mix well.

Press into a 9x13-inch baking pan. Melt the chocolate and butterscotch chips in microwave until smooth. While hot, pour chocolate/butterscotch mixture over mixture in pan.

Chocolate Oatmeal Bars

1 cup all-purpose flour
1 cup butter
1/2 cup brown sugar
1/2 cup granulated sugar
1/2 teaspoon cinnamon
1 1/2 teaspoons vanilla
1 egg
1 1/4 cups quick oats
3/4 cup walnuts, divided
2 cups chocolate chips, divided

Combine all ingredients except half of the chocolate chips and nuts. Pour into a 9x13" baking pan. Bake in a preheated oven at 350 degrees F. for 22 to 28 minutes.

Immediately sprinkle remaining chocolate chips and nuts on top.

Chocolate Chip Fudge Bars

1 (12 oz.) package semi-sweet chocolate chips
3 tablespoons margarine
1 (14 oz.) can sweetened condensed milk
3/4 cup nuts
2 teaspoons vanilla

Melt chocolate chips, margarine and condensed milk together in a saucepan over low heat or in a microwave-safe bowl in microwave. Add nuts and vanilla. Let cool.

Crust:

1/4 cup nuts
1 cup margarine
2 cups brown sugar, packed
1 teaspoon baking soda
2 eggs
3 cups quick cooking oats
1 teaspoon vanilla
2 1/2 cups all-purpose flour
1 teaspoon salt

In a large bowl, combine all crust ingredients. Press 2/3 of the crust mixture into a greased 9x13-inch baking pan. Pour fudge mixture over crust. Use last 1/3 of crust mixture, and dollop "blobs" of mixture over fudge layer. Bake in preheated oven at 350 degrees F. for 20 to 25 minutes.

Mounds Cookie Bars

2 cups graham crackers, crushed
1 cup butter or margarine, melted
1/2 cup confectioners' sugar
2 cups coconut
1 cup sweetened condensed milk
3 (1.55 oz. each) chocolate candy bars
1 cup semi-sweet chocolate chips

In a large bowl, mix graham crackers, melted butter or margarine and confectioners' sugar. Press mixture into a 9x13-inch baking pan. Bake in preheated oven at 350 degrees F. for 10 minutes.

In a medium bowl, combine coconut and sweetened condensed milk; pour over cooled crust. Bake another 10 minutes at 350 degrees F. Melt chocolate candy bars and chocolate chips. Spread on baked crust. Cut into small squares.

Chocolate Turtle Bars

1 (16.5 oz.) package German chocolate cake mix
3/4 cup margarine or butter, melted
2/3 cup evaporated milk, divided
1 cup nuts
1 cup semi-sweet chocolate chips
1 (14 oz.) package caramels

Combine cake mix, margarine or butter and 1/3 cup evaporated milk. Fold in nuts. Stir by hand until dough holds together (fudge-like consistency).

Spread half of the dough in a 9x13-inch baking pan. Bake in preheated oven at 350 degrees F. for 6 minutes. Remove from oven. Sprinkle with chocolate chips.

In a saucepan, combine caramels and 1/3 cup evaporated milk. Cook over medium-low heat until melted. Drizzle melted caramel mixture over chocolate chips. Dot remaining cake batter on top of caramel mixture. Bake at 350 degrees F. for 20 minutes. Cool slightly before cutting into bars.

Chocolate-Peanut Butter Pile-Up

1 cup peanut butter
1 egg
1/2 cup granulated sugar
1 (4 oz.) pkg. baking sweet chocolate, broken in pieces or 1 small pkg. chocolate chips

In a medium bowl, combine peanut butter, egg and sugar. Press or roll dough into a 10 x 7-inch rectangle on an ungreased baking sheet. Bake in preheated oven at 325 degrees for 20 minutes.

Remove from oven. Immediately sprinkle chocolate on top and cover lightly with aluminum foil. Let it stand 2 or 3 minutes; remove foil. Spread chocolate over entire surface and cut into 2 x 1-inch bars. Cool.

Yield: 30 candies.

Cherry Brownie Bars

1 (16.5 oz.) package chocolate cake mix
1 (21 oz.) can of cherry pie filling
2 eggs

Combine cake mix, pie filling and eggs in a large bowl. Beat with electric mixer at medium speed for 5 minutes. Pour into a 9x13-inch baking pan sprayed with non-stick cooking spray. Bake in preheated oven at 350 degrees F. for 35 to 40 minutes. Frost when cool.

Peanut Butter Chocolate Chip Bars

1 (16.5 oz.) package yellow cake mix
1/3 cup vegetable oil
2 eggs
1/2 cup chunky peanut butter
1 cup semi-sweet chocolate chips

In a large bowl, combine cake mix, vegetable oil and eggs. Stir in peanut butter. Add chocolate chips; stir until mixed.

Pat mixture into a 9x13-inch baking pan sprayed with nonstick cooking spray. Bake in preheated oven 14 to 17 minutes at 350 degrees F. or until golden brown.

No Bake Chocolate Crunch Bars

1 cup corn syrup
1 cup granulated sugar
6 cups crisp rice cereal
1 cup peanut butter
1 cup butterscotch chips
1 cup chocolate chips

Mix the syrup and sugar in a saucepan. Cook over medium heat, stirring until it begins to boil. Remove pan from heat. Add the peanut butter to the pan. Mix in the crisp rice cereal.

Press the mix into a buttered or greased 9 x 13" pan. In a microwave, melt the chocolate and butterscotch chips, stirring every 30 seconds until melted. Spread on top of bars.

Chocolate Pecan Bars

1 1/4 cups all-purpose flour
1 cup confectioners' sugar
1/2 cup cocoa
1 cup cold butter or margarine
1 (14 oz.) can sweetened condensed milk
1 egg
2 teaspoons vanilla
1 cup pecans, chopped

In a large bowl, combine flour, sugar, and cocoa; cut in butter or margarine until crumbly (mixture will be dry). Press firmly on bottom of 13x9" baking dish. Bake in preheated oven at 350 degrees F. for 15 minutes. (325 degrees F. for glass dish)

Meanwhile, in a medium bowl, beat milk, egg, and vanilla; mix well. Stir in nuts. Spread evenly over crust. Bake for additional 25 minutes at 350 degrees F. or until lightly browned. Cool. Cut into bars. Store covered in refrigerator.

Yield: 24 to 36 bars.

Chocolatey Bars

1 cup margarine, melted
2 cups brown sugar
2 eggs
2 1/2 cups all-purpose flour
2 teaspoons vanilla
1 teaspoon baking soda
1/8 teaspoon salt
1 cup quick cooking oats
12 oz. chocolate chips
1 (14 oz.) can sweetened condensed milk
2 tablespoons margarine
1/8 teaspoon salt

In a large bowl, combine margarine, brown sugar, eggs, flour, vanilla, baking soda, salt and oats. Spread 2/3 of batter on a greased 11 x 15-inch baking pan.

Melt chocolate chips, condensed milk, margarine and salt together and spread over batter. Drop remainder of dough by spoonfuls on the top. Bake in a preheated oven at 350 degrees F. for 20 minutes.

Toffee Bars

20 graham crackers
1/2 cup butter or margarine
1/2 cup brown sugar, packed
1/2 cup nuts, chopped
3/4 cup chocolate chips

Line a cookie sheet with graham cracker pieces. In a medium saucepan over medium heat, bring butter or margarine and brown sugar to a slow boil. Let boil for two minutes.

Pour sugar mixture over graham crackers. Sprinkle with nuts. Bake in preheated oven at 350 degrees F. for 7 minutes. Remove from oven and immediately sprinkle with chocolate chips. Let cool.

SAUCES, MOUSSES PUDDINGS

SAUCES, MOUSSES, PUDDINGS

Yummy Chocolate Mocha Sauce

1 (12 oz.) package semi-sweet chocolate morsels
1/2 cup butter or margarine
1 cup white corn syrup
4 teaspoons instant coffee, granules
1/8 teaspoon salt
2 cups confectioners' sugar
1 cup hot water
2 teaspoons vanilla

In a double boiler, melt chocolate and butter or margarine together over hot water. Add corn syrup, coffee, and salt. Add sugar and hot water alternately, stirring after each addition. Add vanilla. Serve at once or store in a jar in refrigerator and heat later to serve.

Yield: 4 cups.

Chocolate Fudge Sauce

2 (1 oz. each) squares unsweetened chocolate
1 cup granulated sugar
1/2 cup butter
1/8 teaspoon salt
1 teaspoon vanilla
1 (13 oz.) can evaporated milk

Melt chocolate, sugar, and butter in a double boiler. Add salt, vanilla and evaporated milk. Mix well. Place top of double boiler directly on heat. Bring to a boil, stirring constantly. Boil until mixture thickens, approximately 5 minutes. Serve warm over ice cream. This will keep for 2 to 3 weeks in the refrigerator. Reheat before serving.

Yield: 2 cups.

Oven Fudge Batter Pudding

1 cup all-purpose flour
1/2 cup brown sugar, packed
1/2 cup nuts, chopped
3 tablespoons cocoa
2 teaspoons baking powder
1/2 teaspoon salt
1/2 cup milk
2 tablespoons vegetable oil
1 teaspoon vanilla
Half-and-half (for serving)

Cocoa Syrup:

1/2 cup brown sugar, packed
1/4 cup cocoa
1 2/3 cups hot water
1 teaspoon vanilla

In a large bowl, stir together flour, brown sugar, nuts, cocoa, baking powder, and salt. In another bowl, combine milk, vegetable oil and vanilla; stir into dry mixture until well blended. Pour into a greased 2-quart casserole dish; set aside.

Cocoa Syrup: In medium bowl, combine brown sugar and cocoa; stir in hot water and vanilla until smooth and well blended. Pour Cocoa Syrup on top of mixture in casserole.

Wipe edges of casserole dish clean and bake in preheated oven 350 degrees F. oven for 40 minutes or until toothpick comes out clean. Serve warm in bowls, spooning a portion of cake with syrup. Pour half and half over top.

Yield: 6 servings.

Chocolate Pudding

2/3 cup granulated sugar
1/3 cup cocoa
2 tablespoons cornstarch
2 cups milk
2 beaten egg yolks or 1 beaten egg
2 tablespoons butter
1 teaspoon vanilla

Combine sugar, cocoa, and cornstarch in a 1-1/2 qt. casserole dish. Blend together. Gradually stir milk into cornstarch mixture with wire whisk. Microwave on High for 6-8 minutes, or until thickened and bubbling. Stir 2 to 3 times during cooking time.

Beat half of hot mixture into egg yolks. Return egg mixture to hot mixture. Cook on full power for 1 to 2 minutes, or until thickened and heated through. Stir twice during cooking time. Mix well with wire whisk, stirring in butter and vanilla. Pour into four (6 oz.) custard cups or dessert dishes.

Yield: 4 servings.

Quick Chocolate Mousse

2 eggs
2 egg yolks
1/4 teaspoon salt
6 oz. semi-sweet chocolate, melted and cooled
1/2 cup heavy cream
2 teaspoons vanilla or 4 teaspoons brandy or light rum
Whipped cream

In mixing bowl, beat eggs, yolks, and salt until fluffy. Add chocolate and beat until well blended. Add heavy cream and vanilla and beat until mixture mounds and is smooth. Spoon into serving bowl or 4 individual dessert dishes; chill. Garnish with dollop of whipped cream.

Yield: 4 servings.

Hot Fudge Pudding

1 cup self-rising flour
1 3/4 cups granulated sugar, divided
1/4 cup cocoa, divided
1/2 cup milk
2 tablespoons butter, melted
1 teaspoon vanilla extract
1/8 teaspoon of salt
1 1/2 cups hot water
Whipped cream or ice cream (optional)

In a large bowl, combine flour, 3/4 cup sugar, and 2 tablespoons cocoa; stir in milk, butter, and vanilla. Pour mixture into a 9" square baking pan.

Combine remaining cup of sugar, remaining 2 tablespoons cocoa, and salt; sprinkle over flour mixture. Pour water over top; bake in preheated oven at 350 degrees F. for 30 minutes. Serve warm with whipped cream or ice cream, if desired.

Yield: 6 servings.

Chocolate Meringue

2 egg whites
1/8 teaspoon cream of tartar
1/8 teaspoon salt
1 teaspoon vanilla
3/4 cup granulated sugar
3 oz. chocolate chips

Beat egg whites and cream of tartar until stiff. Add salt, vanilla and sugar until egg whites are stiff and peaked. Add chocolate chips. Drop by teaspoonful on cookie sheet lined with parchment paper. Bake in preheated oven for 25 minutes at 300 degrees F.

Yield: 2 dozen.

Cupcakes
and
Muffins

CUPCAKES and MUFFINS

Brownie Mini Cupcakes

1/4 cup margarine
2 egg whites
1 egg
3/4 cup granulated sugar
2/3 cup all-purpose flour
1/3 cup cocoa
1/4 teaspoon salt
1/2 teaspoon baking powder

In a small saucepan over low heat, melt margarine; cool slightly. In a mixer bowl, on medium speed of electric mixer, beat egg whites and egg until foamy. Add sugar and beat until somewhat thickened.

In a medium bowl, mix together flour, cocoa, salt and baking powder; add to sugar mixture and beat until blended. Gradually add margarine and beat just until mixed well.

Fill muffin cups lined with paper cupcake liners two-thirds full of batter. Bake in preheated oven at 350 degrees F. for 16 to 18 minutes or until inserted toothpick comes out clean. Cool completely then frost.

Yield: 24 mini cupcakes.

Chocolate Cupcakes

1/2 cup butter or margarine, softened
1 cup granulated sugar
1 teaspoon vanilla
4 eggs
1 1/4 cups all-purpose flour
3/4 teaspoon baking soda
1 1/2 cups chocolate syrup

Cream butter or margarine, sugar and vanilla in large mixing bowl until light and fluffy. Add eggs; beat well. Combine flour and baking soda; add alternately with chocolate syrup to creamed mixture. Fill muffin cups that are lined with paper cupcake liners half full of batter.

Bake in preheated oven at 375 degrees F. for 15 to 20 minutes or until inserted toothpick comes out clean. Cool; frost as desired.

Yield: 30 cupcakes.

Chocolate Oatmeal Cupcakes

1 1/2 cups all-purpose flour
1 teaspoon baking powder
1/2 teaspoon baking soda
1/2 teaspoon salt
1/4 cup butter or margarine, softened
1 cup granulated sugar
2 eggs, beaten
1 teaspoon vanilla extract
1 (3 oz.) bar unsweetened chocolate, melted and cooled
2/3 cup buttermilk
1/2 cup rolled oats

Combine flour, baking powder, baking soda and salt; set aside. Cream butter and sugar, until fluffy and light; add eggs and vanilla. Stir in chocolate; mix well. Add flour mixture and buttermilk; stir until well blended. Stir in oats. Fill muffin cups lined with paper cupcake liners two-thirds full of batter.

Bake in preheated oven at 375 degrees F. for 12 minutes or until inserted toothpick comes out clean. Cool, frost each with 1 tablespoon frosting and top with nut half or skip frosting and nut halves and sprinkle with confectioners' sugar.

Yield: 16 cupcakes.

Holiday Cupcakes

1 cup hot water
1 cup chopped dates
1 teaspoon baking soda
1 cup granulated sugar
1/2 cup vegetable oil
1 egg
1/2 teaspoon salt
1 teaspoon vanilla
2 cups all-purpose flour
1/2 cup chocolate chips
1/2 cup chopped nuts (optional)

In a large bowl, combine hot water, dates and baking soda. Let cool. Mix sugar and vegetable oil; add to date mixture. Add egg, salt, vanilla and flour to mixture; mix well. Add chocolate chips and optional nuts.

Fill muffin cups lined with paper cupcake liners two-thirds full of batter. Bake in preheated oven at 350 degrees F for 30 to 35 minutes. Yield: 24 cupcakes.

Peppermint Frosting:
1/2 cup margarine or butter, softened
1 (16-oz.) package confectioners' sugar
1/3 cup milk
1/4 teaspoon peppermint oil

With an electric mixer at medium speed, beat margarine or butter until creamy; slowly add confectioners' sugar alternately with milk. Beat at low speed just until blended after each addition. Stir in peppermint oil. Yield: about 3 cups.

Mini Cream Cheese Cupcakes

Chocolate Cake:
1 cup granulated sugar
1 1/2 cups all-purpose flour
1/3 cup cocoa
1 cup water
1 tablespoon vinegar
1/2 cup vegetable oil
1 teaspoon baking soda
1 teaspoon vanilla

Filling:
8 oz. cream cheese
1 egg
1/3 cup granulated sugar
6 oz. chocolate chips

Filling: In a large bowl, combine cream cheese, egg and sugar; mix with electric mixer until well combined. Stir in chocolate chips.

In a separate large bowl, combine the chocolate cake ingredients. Beat until smooth. Fill cupcake pans half full of the chocolate cake mixture. Top with the cream cheese filling. Bake in a preheated 350 degree F. oven for 16 to 17 minutes if using mini-cupcake pans, or 22 minutes if using regular cupcake pans.

Chocolate Toffee Muffins

1 1/4 cups milk
1 egg
1/3 cup vegetable oil
2 cups all-purpose flour
2/3 cup granulated sugar
1/3 cup cocoa
2 teaspoons baking powder
1/2 teaspoon salt
3 bars chocolate-covered English toffee candy (1.4 oz. each)

In a large bowl, combine milk, egg and oil; beat well by hand. Add flour, sugar, cocoa, baking powder and salt; mix just until dry ingredients are moistened. Chop each candy bar into small pieces. Set aside 1/4 cup of toffee candy; mix remaining candy pieces into batter.

Grease bottoms only of muffin cups or line with paper baking cups. Divide batter evenly among muffin cups. Sprinkle each muffin with the reserved candy. Bake in preheated oven at 400 degrees F. for 18 to 20 minutes, or until inserted toothpick comes out clean.

Yield: 12 muffins.

Banana Chocolate Chip Muffins

2 bananas, extra ripe
2 eggs
1 cup brown sugar
1/2 cup butter, melted
1 teaspoon vanilla
2 1/4 cups all-purpose flour
1/2 teaspoon cinnamon
1/2 teaspoon salt
2 teaspoons baking powder
1 cup chocolate chips
1/2 cup walnuts, chopped

In a medium bowl, mash bananas. Blend in eggs, brown sugar, butter and vanilla.

In a large bowl, combine flour, cinnamon, salt and baking powder; make a well in the center. Pour the banana mixture in the well and mix just to blend. Stir in chocolate chips and nuts.

Spoon into 12 well-greased 2 1/2 inch muffin pan cups or use paper cupcake liners. Bake in preheated oven at 350 degrees F. for 25 to 30 minutes.

Macadamia Nut Muffins

2 cups all-purpose flour
1/2 cup granulated sugar
1 teaspoon baking powder
1/2 teaspoon baking soda
1/2 teaspoon salt
3/4 cup sour cream
1/2 cup margarine or butter, melted
1/4 cup milk
1 tablespoon vanilla
1 egg
1/2 cup macadamia nuts, chopped
1/2 cup miniature semi-sweet chocolate chips

Streusel:
1/4 cup flour
1/4 cup brown sugar, firmly packed
2 tablespoons margarine or butter

In a small bowl, combine all streusel ingredients; blend with fork until mixture resembles coarse crumbs. Set aside.

In large bowl, combine flour, sugar, baking powder, baking soda and salt; mix well. Add sour cream, 1/2 cup margarine or butter, milk, vanilla and egg to flour mixture; stir just until moistened. Fold in macadamia nuts and chocolate chips.

Grease muffin cups or line with paper cupcake liners and fill 3/4 full of batter. Sprinkle each with 1 1/2 teaspoons streusel. Bake in preheated oven at 375 degrees F. for 18 to 20 minutes or until inserted toothpick comes out clean.

Yield: 18 muffins.

S'more Cupcakes

2/3 cup vegetable oil
1 1/2 cups granulated sugar
3 large eggs
1 1/2 cups graham cracker crumbs
1 1/2 cups all-purpose flour
2 teaspoons baking powder
1 teaspoon salt
1 1/4 cups milk
1 teaspoon vanilla
24 chocolate kisses, removed from foil
4 cups miniature marshmallows

With an electric mixer, beat vegetable oil at medium speed. Add sugar gradually, mixing well. Add eggs, one at a time, beating after each addition.

In another bowl, combine graham cracker crumbs, flour, baking powder and salt; add flour mixture to sugar mixture alternately with milk. Beat until well mixed after each addition. Stir in vanilla.

Fill muffin cups lined with paper cupcake liners with 1/4 cup of batter in each cup. Bake in preheated oven at 350 degrees F. for 18 minutes or until done.

Immediately embed a chocolate kiss in the center of each cupcake; followed by 4 or 5 marshmallows, gently pushing into the soft chocolate.

Yield: 24 cupcakes.

Kid Pleasin' Cupcakes

1 (4 oz.) package instant pistachio pudding mix
1 3/4 cups all-purpose flour
3/4 cup mini chocolate chips
2/3 cup granulated sugar
1/2 teaspoon salt
2 1/2 teaspoons baking powder
1 1/4 cups milk
1/2 cup vegetable oil
1 teaspoon vanilla
2 eggs, beaten
1/2 cup candy coated milk chocolate pieces

In a large bowl, combine pudding mix, flour, chocolate chips, sugar, salt and baking powder. In a small bowl, mix together milk, oil, vanilla and eggs. Stir into flour mixture just until well mixed.

Fill muffin cups lined with paper cupcake liners two-thirds full of batter. Bake in a preheated 375 degrees F. oven for 18 to 20 minutes or until golden brown. Cool and frost. Sprinkle with milk chocolate pieces.

Yield: 18 cupcakes.

COOKIES

COOKIES

Perfect Chocolate Cookies

2 tablespoons butter
1 1/2 cups of chocolate chips
1 cup all-purpose flour
1 (14 oz.) can sweetened condensed milk
1 cup pecans

Melt butter and chocolate chips in microwave in a medium bowl. In a large bowl, mix flour, sweetened condensed milk and pecans. Add butter and chocolate chip mixture.

Spray a cookie sheet with non-stick cooking spray. Drop by spoonfuls on a baking sheet and flatten a little. Bake in preheated oven for exactly 10 minutes at 325 degrees F.

Yield: 2 dozen cookies.

Chocolate-Glazed Shortbread Cookie

1 cup confectioners' sugar
1 cup butter or margarine
2 cups all-purpose flour
2 cups almonds or pecans, finely chopped
6 oz. semi-sweet chocolate

In a large bowl, cream confectioners' sugar and butter or margarine; gradually add flour, stir in half the nuts. Chill dough for one hour.

Preheat oven to 325 degrees F. Form I tablespoon of dough into a 2-inch long finger. Cut in half lengthwise and place cut side down on ungreased cookie sheet. Bake in preheated oven 15 minutes at 325 degrees F. or until cookies are pale golden brown. Cool. Melt chocolate. Dip one end of cookie into chocolate then into chopped nuts. Cool on waxed paper until set.

Yield: 5 to 6 dozen.

Chocolate Double Delights

1 1/2 cups brown sugar, packed
3/4 cup butter or margarine
2 tablespoons water
12 oz. package semi-sweet chocolate chips
2 eggs
3 cups all-purpose flour
1 1/4 teaspoons baking soda
1 teaspoon salt

In a medium saucepan, combine brown sugar and butter or margarine over medium heat until melted. Remove from heat and stir in water and chocolate chips. Beat in eggs. Stir in flour, baking soda and salt.

Drop by teaspoonful on ungreased cookie sheet. Bake in preheated oven at 350 degrees F. for 10 minutes. If desired, frost with vanilla frosting, colored pink with peppermint flavoring.

Yield: 5 dozen.

Chocolate Pudding Cookies

1 cup butter, melted
1 teaspoon vanilla
3/4 cup brown sugar, packed
1/4 cup granulated sugar
1 (3.4 oz.) package instant vanilla pudding
2 eggs
2 1/4 cups all-purpose flour
1 teaspoon baking soda
1 cup chopped nuts
2 cups chocolate chips

In a large bowl, combine butter, vanilla, brown sugar, granulated sugar and pudding mix and beat until smooth and creamy. Mix in eggs. Add flour and baking soda, then stir in nuts and chips.

Drop by spoonfuls onto greased baking sheet. Bake in preheated oven at 375 degrees F. for about 10 minutes.

Yield: 7 dozen.

Chow Mein Cookies

1/2 cup peanut butter, chunky
1 cup butterscotch or chocolate chips
1 cup white miniature marshmallows
1-3 oz. can chow mein noodles

In a saucepan over low heat, melt peanut butter and butterscotch or chocolate chips, stirring constantly. (Can also melt in microwave.) Remove from heat; add miniature marshmallows and chow mein noodles. Drop by teaspoonfuls on wax paper or parchment paper. Refrigerate.

Yield: 1 dozen cookies.

Double Chocolate Nuggets

1 package Devils food deluxe cake mix
1/2 cup vegetable oil or canola oil
2 eggs
1 (6 oz.) package semi-sweet chocolate chips
1 teaspoon peppermint extract
1 cup nuts, chopped

In a large bowl, blend together cake mix, oil and eggs. Stir in chocolate chips, peppermint extract and nuts. Drop by teaspoonful onto ungreased cookie sheet. Bake in preheated oven at 350 degrees F. for 10 to 12 minutes, until cookie tests done with a toothpick.

Best Chocolate Chip Cookies

1 cup butter or margarine
1 cup vegetable oil or canola oil
1 cup brown sugar, packed
1 cup granulated sugar
3 1/2 cups all-purpose flour
1 teaspoon salt
1 teaspoon baking soda
1 teaspoon cream of tartar
1 egg
2 teaspoons vanilla
1 teaspoon coconut flavoring
1/2 teaspoon butter flavoring
1 cup oatmeal
1 cup coconut
1 cup crispy rice cereal
12 oz. package semi-sweet chocolate chips

Mix in order given in a large bowl. Drop by tablespoonful onto cookie sheet, press lightly with a fork. Bake in preheated oven at 350 degrees F. for 10 to 12 minutes.

Yield: 6 dozen

Death by Chocolate Cookie

2 pkgs. (16 squares) semi-sweet baking chocolate (divided)
3/4 cup brown sugar, packed
1/4 cup margarine
2 eggs
1 teaspoon vanilla
1/4 teaspoon baking powder
1/2 cup all-purpose flour
2 cups nuts, chopped

Coarsely chop 1 package of chocolate and set aside. Microwave remaining package of chocolate, in 30 second increments, until melted and smooth. Stir in brown sugar, margarine, eggs and vanilla.

Combine baking powder and flour. Mix in reserved chopped chocolate and nuts. Drop by 1/4 measuring cup full onto ungreased cookie sheet. Bake in preheated oven at 350 degrees F. for 12 minutes or until cookies have puffed up.

Yield: 1 1/2 dozen.

Chocolate Drop Cookies

2 eggs, well beaten
2 cups brown sugar, packed
2 teaspoons vanilla
1 cup vegetable oil
3 cups all-purpose flour
1/2 teaspoon salt
1 teaspoon baking soda
1/4 cup cocoa
1 cup sweet milk (or buttermilk, makes cookies more tender)
1/2 cup nuts, chopped

In a large bowl, cream eggs and brown sugar until light and fluffy; add vanilla and vegetable oil. Blend well. Add flour, salt, baking soda and cocoa, alternately with milk. Add nuts.

Drop by teaspoonful onto greased baking sheet. Bake in preheated oven at 350 degrees for 8 to 10 minutes.

Cookie Brittle

1 cup butter or margarine
1 1/2 teaspoons vanilla
1 teaspoon salt
1 cup granulated sugar
2 cups all-purpose flour
1/2 cup nuts
1 cup chocolate chips

Mix all ingredients and press evenly into ungreased 15x10-inch pan. Bake at 375 degrees F for 25 minutes. Cool and then break into irregular shapes.

Chocolate Sundae Cookies

1/2 cup vegetable oil
2/3 cup brown sugar, packed
1 egg
1/2 teaspoon baking soda
1 1/2 cups all-purpose flour
1/4 cup maraschino cherry juice
2 tablespoons milk
2 squares unsweetened chocolate, melted
1/2 cup snipped maraschino cherries
1/2 cup nuts, chopped

In a large bowl, cream vegetable oil and brown sugar. Beat in egg, baking soda and flour. Blend well. Add maraschino cherry juice, milk and chocolate. Blend. Stir in cherries and nuts. Drop on cookie sheet and bake in preheated oven at 350 degrees F. until lightly browned.

Icing:

1 – 6 oz. package semi-sweet chocolate (melted)
1/4 cup vegetable oil
2 dozen large marshmallows, cut in half

Melt chocolate and vegetable oil in double boiler over low heat. Place half of marshmallows, cut side down, on top of each cookie. Dribble hot icing over each cookie to resemble a small chocolate sundae. Cookies must be iced while hot.

Dark Chocolate Chunk Cookies

2 1/2 cups all-purpose flour
1 teaspoon salt
1 teaspoon baking soda
1 3/4 cups granulated sugar
1 cup butter, melted
2 eggs
1 teaspoon pure vanilla extract
2 cups dark chocolate chunks (break up large candy bars)

In a large bowl, mix together flour, baking soda, and salt until well combined. In another bowl, cream butter with sugar until fluffy and light. Add eggs and vanilla; mix well. Stir in dry ingredients until just combined. Mix in chocolate chunks.

Using a cookie scoop, make large dough balls and place on cookie sheets lined with parchment paper. Bake in preheated oven at 375 degrees F. for 10 to 13 minutes until cookies are golden around the edges.

Forgotten Cookies

2 egg whites
2/3 cup granulated sugar
1 teaspoon vanilla
1 (6 oz.) package chocolate chips
1/2 cup pecans, chopped

Preheat oven to 350 degrees F. In a large bowl, beat egg whites, sugar and vanilla until stiff, then stir in chocolate chips and pecans.

Drop by teaspoonfuls on greased cookie sheet. Place cookies in a 350 degree F. oven and turn off oven. Leave cookies in oven overnight and do not open oven until the next morning.

Yield: 2 dozen.

The "Big" Chocolate Chip Cookie

1/2 cup butter
3/4 cup brown sugar, packed
3 tablespoons granulated sugar
1 teaspoon vanilla
1 egg
1 1/2 cups all-purpose flour
3/4 teaspoon baking soda
1/2 teaspoon salt
1/2 cup semi-sweet chocolate chips

In a large bowl, cream butter with brown sugar and granulated sugar. Add vanilla and egg.

In another bowl, mix together flour, baking soda and salt. Add to creamed mixture. Add chocolate chips. Chill dough for 45 minutes in the freezer or 1 1/2 hours in the refrigerator.

Pat dough within 1/2 inch of the edge of a regular-size pizza pan. Bake in preheated oven 13 minutes at 350 degrees. (Cookie must be golden brown across the entire cookie, or it will be doughy in the center.)

Pumpkin Spice Iced Cookies

1 cup granulated sugar
1 cup margarine, softened
1 (16 oz.) can solid-pack pumpkin
2 eggs
1 teaspoon vanilla
2 1/4 cups all-purpose flour
1/2 teaspoon baking soda
1 teaspoon baking powder
1/2 teaspoon salt
1 1/2 teaspoons pumpkin pie spice
1 cup walnuts, chopped
1 (12 oz.) package semi-sweet chocolate chips

Glaze:
1 cup confectioners' sugar
1 tablespoon milk
1/2 teaspoon vanilla

In a large bowl, beat sugar and margarine until creamy. Add pumpkin, eggs and vanilla. In a separate bowl, combine flour, baking soda, baking powder, salt and pumpkin pie spice. Add to sugar mixture; mix well.

Stir in nuts and chocolate chips. Drop cookies by teaspoonfuls on greased cookie sheets. Bake in preheated oven at 350 degrees F for 13 to 15 minutes, or until edges are lightly browned. Let stand for 5 minutes. Remove from cookie sheet and cool. Combine glaze ingredients and spread on baked cookies.

Yield: 5 1/2 dozen.

Cranberry-Chocolate Chippers

3/4 cup + 2 tablespoons butter, softened
2/3 cup granulated sugar
1 cup brown sugar, packed
1 egg
1/2 teaspoon vanilla extract
2 teaspoons orange zest, finely chopped
1/2 teaspoon salt
3/4 teaspoon baking soda
2 cups all-purpose flour
1 cup quick-cooking oats
3/4 cup sweetened coconut
1 1/2 cups dried cranberries or whole fresh cranberries
1 1/2 cups chocolate chunks (dark, white or milk chocolate)

In a medium mixing bowl, cream butter, sugar, and brown sugar for 2 to 3 minutes. Beat in egg and vanilla extract. Add orange zest. Stir in salt, baking soda and flour until combined. Fold in oats, coconut, cranberries and chocolate chunks.

Drop dough by teaspoonful 2 inches apart on a parchment-lined baking sheet. Bake in preheated oven at 375 degrees F. for 8 to 10 minutes. Transfer cookies to a wire rack.

Yield: 48 cookies.

Norwegian Chocolate Wafers

1/3 cup butter, softened
2 hard-cooked egg yolks, sieved
1/4 cup granulated sugar
1 teaspoon vanilla
1 cup all-purpose flour
1/2 cup semi-sweet chocolate chips, ground

In a large bowl, combine butter, egg yolks, sugar and vanilla; blend well. Add flour and ground chocolate chips; mix well.

Roll dough between 2 sheets of wax paper to 1/4-inch thickness. Cut into 2-inch circles and bake on greased cookie sheet in preheated oven at 400 degrees F for 8 minutes.

Yield: 2 dozen.

Cracker Jack Cookies

1 cup granulated sugar
1 cup brown sugar
1 cup butter
2 eggs
2 teaspoons vanilla
1 1/2 cups all-purpose flour
1 teaspoon baking powder
1 teaspoon baking soda
1 cup coconut
2 cups quick oats
2 cups crisp rice cereal
1 cup semi-sweet chocolate chips

In a large bowl, cream together granulated sugar, brown sugar and butter. Add eggs and vanilla; mix well.

Combine flour, baking soda, and baking powder and beat into creamed mixture. Add coconut, oats, crisp rice cereal and chocolate chips, in that order. Drop onto cookie sheet and bake in preheated oven at 350 degrees F. for 10 to 12 minutes.

Peanut Butter and Chocolate Cookies

1 large egg, beaten
1 cup crunchy peanut butter
1 cup granulated sugar
36 milk chocolate kisses, unwrapped

In a large bowl, combine egg, peanut butter and sugar; shape into 3/4-inch balls. Place on ungreased cookie sheets; bake in preheated oven at 350 degrees F. for 10 minutes.

Remove from oven and quickly press a chocolate kiss in the center of each cookie; remove to wire racks to cool.

Yield: 3 dozen.

Easy Chocolate Crinkle Cookies

1 box Devils food chocolate cake mix
1 egg
4 oz. refrigerated whipped topping
Confectioners' sugar

In a medium bowl, mix cake mix, egg and refrigerated whipped topping; form into little balls. Roll balls in confectioners' sugar. Bake in preheated oven at 350 degrees for 10 minutes.

Chocolate-Walnut Drop Cookies

1/2 cup butter or margarine, softened
1 cup granulated sugar
2 eggs
1 teaspoon vanilla
1/8 teaspoon salt
2 oz. unsweetened chocolate, melted and cooled
1 cup all-purpose flour
1/2 cup walnuts, chopped
Confectioners' sugar

In a large mixer bowl, cream butter or margarine, sugar, eggs, vanilla, and salt until light and fluffy. Beat in chocolate until well blended. Stir in flour and nuts. Drop by heaping teaspoonful 2" apart on well-greased cookie sheet.

Bake in preheated 350 degrees F. oven for 10 minutes or until edges are crisp. Cool 1 minute before removing to rack to cool. Sprinkle confectioners' sugar on warm cookies.

Yield: 4 dozen.

Chocolate Banana Cookies

2/3 cup vegetable oil
1 cup granulated sugar
2 eggs
1 (6 oz.) package semi-sweet chocolate chips
1 teaspoon vanilla
2 1/4 cups all-purpose flour
2 teaspoons baking powder
1/2 teaspoon salt
1/4 teaspoon baking soda
1 cup mashed bananas

In a large bowl, cream vegetable oil and sugar. Add eggs, one at a time, beating after each addition. Stir in chocolate chips and vanilla.

Mix flour, baking powder, salt and baking soda and add to creamed mixture alternately with mashed bananas. Drop by teaspoonful onto ungreased cookie sheet. Bake in preheated oven at 350 degrees F. for 12 to 15 minutes.

No-Bake Chocolate Oatmeal Cookies

1/2 cup butter
2 cups granulated sugar
3 tablespoons cocoa
1 cup peeled and grated apple
1/8 teaspoon salt
3 cups regular rolled oats
1 cup pecans, chopped
1 teaspoon vanilla extract
1/2 cup coconut (optional)
Confectioners' sugar

Melt butter in a large saucepan. Add sugar, cocoa, apple and salt. Combine thoroughly. Bring mixture to a boil and boil 1 minute. Remove from heat.

Immediately add oats, nuts, vanilla, and optional coconut. Mix well. Drop by teaspoons onto wax paper. When cool, roll in confectioners' sugar.

Yield: 5 to 6 dozen.

Chocolate Macaroons

2 egg whites
1 cup granulated sugar
1/8 teaspoon salt
1/2 teaspoon vanilla
1 1/2 cups shredded coconut
2 (1 oz. each) semi-sweet chocolate baking squares

In a large bowl, beat egg whites; add sugar, salt, vanilla and coconut. Melt chocolate and add to mixture. Drop by teaspoonful on greased cookie sheet; Bake in preheated oven at 250 degrees F. for 20 minutes or less. (Be sure cookies don't dry out in oven)

Chocolate Mint Cookies

3/4 cup margarine
1 1/2 cups brown sugar, packed
2 tablespoons water
2 cups semi-sweet chocolate chips
2 eggs, beaten
2 1/2 cups all-purpose flour plus 2 tablespoons
1 1/4 teaspoons baking soda
1/2 teaspoon salt
3 pkgs. Andes mints

In a large saucepan, heat margarine, brown sugar and water over low heat until margarine is melted. Add chocolate chips and stir until melted. Cool for 10 minutes. Add eggs; then add flour, baking soda and salt. Chill at least 1 hour.

Roll into balls and bake in preheated oven at 350 degrees F. for 9 to 10 minutes. Put Andes mints on top as soon as removed from oven. Let melt and spread over top of cookie.

Yield: 6 dozen.

Whirligig Refrigerator Cookies

1/2 cup butter
1/2 cup brown sugar
1/2 cup granulated sugar
1/2 cup cream peanut butter
1 egg
1 1/4 cups all-purpose flour
1/2 teaspoon baking soda
1/2 teaspoon salt
1 cup chocolate chips

In a large bowl, cream butter, brown sugar, granulated sugar and peanut butter. Mix in egg. Combine the flour, salt and baking soda; add to the creamed mixture.

Roll the dough into an oblong shape, about 1/4 inch thick. (Hint: Roll dough between 2 floured sheets of wax paper.) Melt chocolate chips in microwave. Spread chocolate on the dough. Roll up the dough jelly-roll fashion.

Chill the dough logs for 20 minutes. Slice 1/4 inch thick pieces and place on cookie sheet. Bake in preheated oven at 375 degrees F. for 6 to 7 minutes.

Bakery Chocolate Chip Cookies

3/4 cup brown sugar, packed
1/3 cup granulated sugar
1/2 cup butter, melted
1 egg
1 egg yolk
2 1/4 teaspoons vanilla
1 1/2 cups all-purpose flour
1/2 teaspoon salt
1/4 teaspoon cinnamon
1/2 teaspoon baking soda
1 1/2 cups semi-sweet chocolate chips or chocolate chunks

In a large bowl, combine brown sugar and granulated sugar. Add melted butter to sugars and mix well. Add egg, egg yolk and vanilla and mix well until light and creamy.

Mix flour, salt, cinnamon and baking soda together; add to egg mixture. Add the chocolate chips. Grease a cookie sheet or use parchment paper. Drop dough by large spoonfuls (bakery style) on a cookie sheet and flatten cookies a bit. Bake in preheated oven at 325 degrees F. for 15 to 16 minutes or until edges are turning light brown.

Cracker Cookies

60 to 70 round buttery crackers
24 oz. chocolate or white almond bark
1 cup peanut butter

Spread peanut butter between 2 crackers (making a small sandwich). Melt almond bark in double boiler. Let it get quite thin. Using tongs, dip cracker sandwich in melted bark. Shake off excess, put on waxed paper to cool.

Yield: 30 to 35 cookies.

Cakes

CAKE

Moist Chocolate Cake

3 cups all-purpose flour
1/2 cup cocoa
2 cups granulated sugar
2 eggs
1 cup vegetable oil
1/2 teaspoon salt
1 teaspoon vanilla
1 cup buttermilk
2 teaspoons baking soda
1 cup boiling water

In a large bowl, mix together flour and cocoa. In another bowl, cream together sugar and eggs. Add vegetable oil, salt and vanilla to sugar and egg mixture; mix well.

To the sugar mixture, add buttermilk alternately with flour mixture and cocoa mixture. Measure baking soda into measuring cup and add enough boiling water to make 1 cup. Pour into batter and mix well. Batter will be very thin. Pour into a greased 9x13-inch baking pan. Bake in preheated oven at 350 degrees F. for 30 to 35 minutes.

Chocolate Chip Cheesecake

Crust:

1 1/2 cups graham cracker crumbs
1/3 cup cocoa
1/3 cup granulated sugar
1/3 cup butter, melted

Filling:

3 (8 oz.) pkgs. cream cheese, softened
1 (14 oz.) can sweetened condensed milk
3 eggs
2 teaspoons vanilla
1 1/2 cups semi-sweet chocolate chips
1 teaspoon all-purpose flour

Mix graham cracker crumbs, cocoa, sugar and butter. Press into bottom of a 9" spring-form pan.

Filling: Beat cream cheese until fluffy. Add sweetened condensed milk, beating until smooth. Add eggs and vanilla; mix well.

In a small resealable bag, combine 1/2 cup chocolate chips with flour. Toss to coat; add floured chips to filling mixture. Pour over crust. Sprinkle remaining 1/2 cup chocolate chips evenly over top.

Bake in preheated oven at 300 degrees F. for 1 hour; turn off oven and allow to cool in oven 1 hour. Remove from oven; cool to room temperature. Refrigerate.

Chocolate Layer Cake

1/2 cup vegetable oil
2 cups granulated sugar
2 eggs
1 teaspoon vanilla
2 cups all-purpose flour
1/3 cup cocoa
2 teaspoons baking powder
1/2 teaspoon baking soda
1/2 teaspoon salt
1 1/2 cups milk

In a large bowl, beat together vegetable oil and sugar. Beat in eggs and vanilla. In another bowl, combine flour, cocoa, baking powder, baking soda and salt. Add to creamed mixture alternating with milk.

Pour into two greased and floured 9" round baking pans. Bake in preheated oven at 350 degrees for 30 to 35 minutes or until done. Cool and frost.

Chocolate Coffee Cake

2 cups granulated sugar
1/2 cup cocoa
1/2 cup vegetable oil
3 eggs, well-beaten
1/2 cup cold black coffee
2 cups all-purpose flour
2 teaspoons baking soda
1 teaspoon vanilla
1/2 teaspoon salt
1 cup boiling water

In a large bowl, combine sugar and cocoa. Blend with vegetable oil. Add eggs and coffee. Mix thoroughly.

Combine flour and baking soda; add gradually to sugar mixture, beating after each addition. Mix in vanilla, salt and hot water. Pour into well-greased 9x13-inch baking pan. Bake in preheated oven at 350 degrees F. for about 40 minutes.

Almond Joy Cake

1 chocolate cake mix with pudding
1 (14 oz.) can condensed milk
2 (3 1/2 oz.) cans coconut
1 (15 oz.) can cream of coconut
1 (12 oz.) carton refrigerated whipped topping

Bake cake as directed on package in a 9x13-inch baking pan. Prick top of cake with handle of a wooden spoon while cake is still hot. Immediately, pour can of milk and 1/2 can cream of coconut over top of cake. Top with 1 can of coconut; cool. When cool, top with whipped topping. Top whipped topping with another can of coconut.

For Easter, sprinkle top with jellybeans and tint coconut in different colors.

Chocolate Salad Dressing Cake

1 cup Miracle Whip
1 cup granulated sugar
2 cups all-purpose flour
4 tablespoons cocoa
2 teaspoons baking soda
1 cup water
1 teaspoon vanilla

Mix all ingredients together in a large bowl. Bake in preheated oven at 350 degrees for 40 minutes.

Heath Cake

1 package white cake mix
1 package chocolate fudge instant pudding
2 cups water
2 egg whites

Frosting:

1 cup confectioners' sugar
1/2 cup soft margarine
2 egg yolks
1 (8 oz.) carton refrigerated whipped topping
2 crushed Heath bars

In a large bowl, mix cake mix, pudding, water and egg whites. Pour into a 9x13-inch baking pan. Bake in preheated oven at 350 degrees for 25 minutes; cool.

Frosting: In a medium bowl, mix sugar, margarine and yolks together and beat. Fold in whipped topping. Frost cooled cake. Sprinkle crushed Heath bars on top. Refrigerate.

Sour Cream Chocolate Cake

1 3/4 cups all-purpose flour
3 rounded tablespoons cocoa
1 teaspoon baking soda
3 eggs
1 1/2 cups granulated sugar
1/2 teaspoon salt
1 1/2 cups sour cream
1 teaspoon vanilla

In a large bowl, mix flour, cocoa and baking soda. Set aside. In another bowl, beat eggs, sugar and salt at high speed. Blend in dry ingredients and sour cream alternating beginning and ending with dry ingredients. Add vanilla and blend well. If batter is too thick, add a little water. It should not be thick for a moist cake.

Pour into a 9x13-inch baking pan. Bake in preheated oven at 350 degrees for 35 minutes.

Yield: Serves 15.

Chocolate Applesauce Cake

1/2 cup margarine
1 1/2 cups granulated sugar
1/2 teaspoon cinnamon
1 1/2 tablespoons cocoa
2 eggs
2 cups all-purpose flour
1/2 teaspoon salt
2 cups applesauce
2 tablespoons granulated sugar
1 to 2 cups semi-sweet chocolate chips

In a large bowl, mix together margarine and sugar. Add cinnamon, cocoa, eggs, flour, salt and applesauce; mix well. Pour in a greased 9x13-inch baking pan.

Sprinkle the batter with 2 tablespoons sugar and 1 to 2 cups chocolate chips. Bake in preheated oven at 350 degrees for 30 to 40 minutes.

Snicker Cake

1 box German chocolate cake mix
1-14 oz. package caramels
1/2 cup butter or margarine
1/3 cup milk
3/4 cup semi-sweet chocolate chips
1 cup pecans

Prepare cake mix as directed on package. Pour half of batter into greased 9x13-inch baking pan. Bake in preheated oven at 350 degrees for 20 minutes.

In a double boiler, melt caramels, butter or margarine and milk together. Remove cake from oven and pour caramel mixture over it. Top with chocolate chips and pecans. Dot remaining cake batter over top and return cake to oven at 250 degrees F. for 20 minutes; then turn oven back up to 350 degrees for 10 to 15 minutes.

Earthquake Cake

1 cup pecans, chopped
1 cup coconut
1 box chocolate cake mix
1 (8 oz.) package cream cheese
4 oz. margarine
1 lb. confectioners' sugar

Grease and flour a 9x13-inch baking pan. Spread pecans and coconuts in the bottom of the pan. Mix cake as directed on package. Spread cake on top of nuts and coconut.

In a medium bowl, mix cream cheese, margarine and confectioners' sugar. Drop by teaspoon on top of the cake mix. Do not stir. Bake in preheated oven for 1 hour at 325 degrees F.

Fudge Cake

3/4 cup butter
2 1/4 cups granulated sugar
1 1/2 teaspoons vanilla
3 eggs
3 (1 oz. each) squares unsweetened chocolate, melted
3 cups all-purpose flour
1 1/2 teaspoons baking soda
3/4 teaspoon salt
1 1/2 cups ice water

In a large bowl, cream butter, sugar and vanilla. Add eggs and beat until fluffy. Add melted chocolate. In another bowl, combine flour, baking soda and salt.

Add the flour mixture to sugar mixture alternating with ice water. Grease 3 9-inch cake pans and line with parchment paper. Bake in preheated oven 30 to 35 minutes at 350 degrees F.

Yield: Serves 12.

Knock Your Socks Off Cake

1 box German chocolate cake mix
8 oz. cream cheese
2 cups semi-sweet chocolate chips
2 teaspoons vanilla
1 cup granulated sugar
2 eggs
1 cup pecans

Prepare cake mix according to directions. Pour into a 9x13-inch baking pan and set aside. Mix rest of ingredients together and drop by teaspoonful on cake batter. Bake in preheated oven at 350 degrees for 40 to 50 minutes.

Frosting:

1 (3 oz.) package instant chocolate pudding
1 package Dream Whip (dry)
1 1/2 cups milk
1 teaspoon vanilla

In a medium bowl, combine all frosting ingredients and whip until thick. Spread on cooled cake. Refrigerate, covered.

Chocolate Ice Box Cake

2 (4 oz. each) bars German sweet chocolate
3 tablespoons hot water
3/4 cup granulated sugar
4 eggs, separated
1 teaspoon vanilla
1 lb. vanilla wafer crumbs
6 tablespoons butter, melted
2 cups whipping cream

Melt chocolate, hot water and sugar in a double boiler. Stir in egg yolks and vanilla. Beat egg whites until stiff and fold into chocolate mixture; set aside to cool.

In a medium bowl, mix vanilla wafer crumbs with melted butter. Line a 9x13-inch baking pan with a layer of vanilla wafer crumbs. Add layer of chocolate and layer of whipped cream. Repeat with another layer. Top with remaining crumbs. Make day before serving.

Yield: Serves 12.

German Chocolate Pound Cake (Bundt Cake)

2 cups granulated sugar
1 cup vegetable oil
4 eggs
2 teaspoons vanilla
2 teaspoons butter flavor
3 cups all-purpose flour
1/2 teaspoon baking soda
1 teaspoon salt
1 (4 oz.) package German sweet chocolate baking bar

In a large bowl, cream sugar and vegetable oil; add eggs, vanilla and butter flavoring. In another bowl, combine flour, baking soda and salt; add to creamed mixture and blend well.

Melt chocolate and add gradually to mixture. Pour into a greased Bundt pan. Bake in preheated oven at 325 degrees F. for 1 hour and 30 minutes. Store tightly covered.

Black Russian Cake
(Bundt Cake)

1 (16.5 oz.) box chocolate cake mix
1/2 cup vegetable oil
1 package instant chocolate pudding mix
4 eggs
1/2 cup cold coffee
3/4 cup Kulua and Crème de Cocoa

Lightly grease a 12 cup Bundt pan or 10 inch Angel pan. Mix cake according to the directions on cake box, substituting liquor for water. Bake in preheated oven at 350 degrees F. for 50 minutes. Let cool for 10 minutes, remove from pan. Poke holes in top with fork and drizzle with glaze below.

Glaze:

1 cup confectioners' sugar
2 tablespoons coffee
2 tablespoons Kulua
2 tablespoons Crème de Cocoa

Combine sugar, coffee, Kulua and Crème de Cocoa. Beat until smooth and drizzle as directed.

Yield: Serves 16.

Chocolate Mayonnaise Cake (Bundt Cake)

1/4 cup cocoa
1 cup real mayonnaise
2 cups all-purpose flour
1 cup granulated sugar
2 teaspoons baking soda
1 cup water, warm
1 teaspoon vanilla flavoring

In a large bowl, combine all ingredients. Mix just long enough to blend together. Pour batter into a greased Bundt pan and bake in a preheated 375 degrees F. oven for 40 minutes. Cake is very moist.

Banana Chocolate Chip Cake (Bundt Cake)

4 cups all-purpose flour
2 teaspoons baking soda
1 teaspoon salt
2 teaspoons baking powder
2 cups granulated sugar
1 cup margarine, softened
4 eggs
1 cup milk
2 teaspoons vanilla
4 bananas, mashed
12 oz. chocolate chips

Grease and dust a Bundt pan with flour. In a large bowl, combine flour, baking soda, salt and baking powder; set aside.

In another bowl, cream sugar and margarine. Add eggs one at a time; beat mixture well after each egg addition. Add creamed mixture to the dry ingredients; add milk and vanilla.

Fold in mashed bananas and chocolate chips. Pour cake batter into Bundt pan. Bake in a preheated 350 degree F. oven for 50 to 60 minutes. Insert toothpick for doneness test. Let cake cool completely then turn out and dust with powder sugar.

Chocolate-Pumpkin Cake (Tube Cake)

Fine dry bread crumbs
2 3/4 cups all-purpose flour
3/4 cup cocoa
2 teaspoons baking powder
1 teaspoon baking soda
1 1/2 teaspoons cinnamon
1/2 teaspoon ginger
1/4 teaspoon cloves
1/4 teaspoon nutmeg
1/2 teaspoon salt
1 cup butter, softened
2 cups granulated sugar
1 1/2 teaspoons vanilla
4 large eggs
16 oz. solid-packed pumpkin
1 1/2 cups walnuts, chopped
Confectioners' sugar (optional)

Place oven rack on bottom third of oven. Preheat oven to 350 degrees F. Thoroughly grease a 12-cup fluted tube pan; sprinkle with bread crumbs.

In a large bowl, combine flour, cocoa, baking powder, baking soda, cinnamon, ginger, cloves, nutmeg and salt.

In another bowl, beat butter, sugar, and vanilla with mixer until light and fluffy. Add eggs one at a time, beating well after each addition. Stir in half the flour mixture, then pumpkin, then remaining flour mixture just until well blended. Stir in walnuts.

Pour batter into prepared pan; smooth top. Bake in preheated oven at 350 degrees F. 80 to 90 minutes or until pick comes out clean. Cool in pan on rack 15 minutes. Invert on rack and remove pan; cool completely. Dust top with confectioners' sugar.

Yield: 16 servings.

Chocolate Zucchini Cake
(Tube Cake)

1 dark chocolate cake mix
1 teaspoon cinnamon
1 1/4 cups water
3 eggs
1/2 cup vegetable oil
1 cup zucchini, shredded and unpeeled
1/4 cup nuts, chopped
Vanilla frosting (optional)

In a large bowl, combine dry cake mix and cinnamon. Add water, eggs and vegetable oil, mix well. With electric mixer, beat for 2 minutes at medium speed. Fold in zucchini.

Grease and flour a 10" tube pan. Pour batter into tube pan and spread evenly. Bake in preheated oven at 350 degrees F. for 50 to 60 minutes. Cool completely before removing from pan. When fully cool, frost with vanilla frosting and sprinkle pecans over top.

Pecan Chocolate Sheet Cake

1/2 cup butter or margarine
4 tablespoons cocoa
1/2 cup vegetable oil
1 cup water
2 cups all-purpose flour
2 cups granulated sugar
2 beaten eggs
1/2 cup buttermilk
1 teaspoon baking soda
1 teaspoon vanilla
1 cup chopped pecans

In a medium saucepan, bring butter or margarine, cocoa, vegetable oil and water to boil. Remove from heat and add remaining ingredients, mix well. Pour into a 16 x 11-inch greased sheet cake pan. Bake in preheated oven for 15 minutes at 400 degrees F.

Yield: Serves 20-24.

Chocolate Sheet Cake

2 cups granulated sugar
2 cups all-purpose flour
1/4 cup cocoa
1 cup water
1/2 cup butter or margarine
1/2 cup vegetable oil
1 1/2 teaspoons baking soda
1/2 cup buttermilk
2 beaten eggs
1 teaspoon vanilla

In a large bowl, combine sugar, flour and cocoa. In a saucepan, bring water, butter or margarine and oil to a boil. Pour over sugar mixture; mix well.

Dissolve baking soda in buttermilk. Add eggs, baking soda mixture and vanilla to cake mixture; mix well. Bake in preheated oven at 350 degrees F. for 20 minutes in a jelly roll pan. Frost while cake is hot.

Frosting:

1/2 cup butter or margarine
1/3 cup buttermilk
1 box confectioners' sugar
1/4 cup cocoa
1 cup nuts, chopped
1 teaspoon vanilla

Mix all ingredients and frost while cake is hot.

Ho-Ho Cake

1 package chocolate cake mix
1 1/4 cups milk
5 tablespoons all-purpose flour
1 teaspoon vanilla
1/2 cup butter or margarine
1/2 cup vegetable oil
1 cup sugar

Prepare chocolate cake mix as directed on package and bake in preheated oven in a jelly roll pan (10 1/2 x 15 1/2 x 1) at 350 degrees F. for 20 to 25 minutes.

In a medium saucepan, combine milk, flour and vanilla; bring to a boil and boil until thick; stirring constantly. Set aside to cool. When cool, beat together butter or margarine, vegetable oil and sugar and add to cooled flour mixture; beat until fluffy. Spread on cake and refrigerate 1 hour.

Frosting

FROSTING

Richmond Chocolate Frosting

1/2 cup granulated sugar
1 1/2 tablespoons cornstarch
1/2 cup boiling water
1/2 teaspoon vanilla
1 oz. chocolate (or 1/4 cup chocolate chips)
1 1/2 tablespoons butter

Combine all ingredients in a medium saucepan; cook over medium heat until thick.

Double recipe for an average cake. Spread while hot. Has consistency of pudding. Works great between cake layers.

Chocolate Frosting

1 cup margarine, softened
5 cups confectioners' sugar
1/3 cup cocoa
1-1 oz. square unsweetened baking chocolate, melted
2 teaspoons vanilla
4 to 6 tablespoons hot water

In a large mixing bowl, cream margarine. Gradually add confectioners' sugar, cocoa, baking chocolate, vanilla and water. Cream until smooth. Frost cake.

"Heaven in a Hurry" Frosting

1 cup semi-sweet chocolate chips
1 cup confectioners' sugar
1/3 cup evaporated milk (try 1/4 cup first and add the rest if
too dry)

In microwave, melt chocolate, stirring every 30 seconds until
melted. Add sugar and milk gradually, alternately, beating
after each addition. Spread immediately.

Reduced-Fat Chocolate Frosting

1/2 cup cottage cheese, 2% low fat
1/4 cup margarine, softened
1/4 cup cocoa
1/4 teaspoon vanilla
2 cups confectioners' sugar

In a blender, blend cottage cheese and margarine until smooth. In a medium bowl, combine cottage cheese mixture, cocoa and vanilla. Gradually beat in confectioners' sugar. Keep frosting refrigerated until use.

Yield: 1 1/2 cups.

Cacao Chocolate Buttercream Frosting

1 (4 oz.) cacao bittersweet chocolate baking bar
1/2 cup butter, softened
1/4 teaspoon vanilla
1 1/3 cups confectioners' sugar

Break the baking bar into small pieces and microwave the chocolate on HIGH for 30 seconds. Stir chocolate and if not completely melted, microwave for 10 to 15 more seconds. Repeat with 10 second intervals until melted. Let cool.

In a medium bowl, beat butter and vanilla until fluffy and light. Beat in chocolate until well blended. Add sugar and beat until fluffy and light again. Add one teaspoon of milk at a time until desired consistency.

Yield: 1 1/2 cups.

BONNIE SCOTT

Other Books by Bonnie Scott

4 Ingredient Cookbook: 150 Quick & Easy Timesaving Recipes
Slow Cooker Comfort Foods
150 Easy Classic Chicken Recipes
Grill It! 125 Easy Recipes
Soups, Sandwiches and Wraps
Simply Fleece
Cookie Indulgence
Bacon Cookbook: 150 Easy Bacon Recipes
Pies and Mini Pies
Holiday Recipes: 150 Easy Recipes and Gifts From Your Kitchen

CAMPING

100 Easy Camping Recipes
Camping Recipes: Foil Packet Cooking

IN JARS

100 Easy Recipes in Jars
100 More Easy Recipes in Jars
Desserts in Jars

All titles available in Paperback and Kindle versions at Amazon.com

44508094R00096

Made in the USA
Columbia, SC
19 December 2018